THE TRUTH ABOUT BAPTISM

(A Study In Baptism & Tongues)

For My Granddaughter, Sarina
I Love You

ISBN: 13: 978-0692451557
ISBN: 10: 0692451552

The Truth About Baptism
Sheila R. Vitale

Living Epistles Ministries
Sheila R. Vitale
P O Box 562
Port Jefferson Station, NY 11776-0562 USA
631-331-1493

Living Epistles Ministries

Sheila R. Vitale

Pastor, Teacher, Founder

PO Box 562

Port Jefferson Station, NY 11776 USA

THE TRUTH ABOUT BAPTISM

(A Study In Baptism & Tongues)

**Is an Edited, Enhanced Transcript of
LEM Message #113**

The Truth About Baptism

(A Study In Baptism & Tongues)

Was Transcribed and Edited For Clarity, Continuity of
Thought, And Punctuation by

The *LEM* Transcribing and Editing Team

And

**Formatted as a book by
The LEM Administrative Professional Staff**

Living Epistles Ministries
~ Judeo-Christian Spiritual Philosophy ~
Sheila R. Vitale
Pastor, Teacher & Founder

Ministry Staff
Anthony Milton, Teacher (South Carolina)
Brooke Paige, Teacher (New York)
Sandra Aldrich (MN) (July 7, 1975 – April 18, 2021)

Administrative Staff
Susan Panebianco, Office Manager

Editorial Staff
Rose Herczeg, Editor

Technical Staff
Lape Mobolaji-Lawal, Database Administrator

Ministry Illustrators
Cecilia H. Bryant (Oct. 18, 1921 – Oct. 23, 2013)
Fidelis Onwubueke

Music Staff
June Eble, Singer, Lyricist and Clarinetist
(July 20, 1931 – Jan. 24, 2024)
Don Gervais, Singer, Lyricist and Guitarist
Rita L. Rora, Singer, Lyricist and Guitarist

Table of Contents

PROLOGUE I

INTRODUCTION III

THREE STAGES OF BAPTISM FOR THE CARNAL MIND 1

TWO STAGES OF HOLY SPIRIT BAPTISM 3

THE CURSE UPON BABEL REVERSED IN THE HOLY SPIRIT 5

JESUS ANOINTED 7

    PUTTING ON CHRIST 9

JOHN'S BAPTISM FOR THE REMISSION OF SIN 11

    WATER BAPTISM 11

    CHRIST VS. CHRIST JESUS 13

    THE GOSPEL OF THE CROSS VS. THE GOSPEL OF PERFECTION 16

    A CALL TO REPENTANCE 17

SPIRITUAL BAPTISM 23

    BAPTISM – AN ACT OF FAITH 25

BAPTISM IN THE NAME OF THE LORD JESUS 27

    THE GOSPEL OF THE CROSS VS. THE GOSPEL OF THE KINGDOM 28

    RECEIVING THE HOLY GHOST 31

    THE VIRILE SEED OF THE LORD JESUS 33

    ASCENSION ABOVE THE SIN NATURE 37

        Ultimate Reconciliation 38

        Reconciled to the Lord Jesus 40

        Spiritual Maturation 41

        Five Virgins 43

        Gospel of Perfection 43

        Spiritual Perfection 47

        Following the Call of God 48

    THE HOLY SPIRIT - A TASTE OF BAPTISM 51

CORNELIUS..52
THE GOSPEL OF THE CROSS IS FOR THE GENTILES 53
THE GOSPEL OF THE KINGDOM IS FOR THE JEW............................53
FIRST FRUITS COMPANY...54
SPIRITUAL INTIMACY 55
CHRIST JESUS IS SAVIOR 56
THE PERSONALITY IS NOT RESURRECTED 57
CHRIST IS THE ONLY REALITY 58
PHYSICAL WATER, SPIRITUAL WATER 59
FILLED WITH THE HOLY GHOST 60
SEIZED BY THE HOLY GHOST...63
    The Seed Of The Manchild 65

TONGUES **67**

TONGUES OF MEN (OTHER TONGUES) 67
TONGUES OF ANGELS (NEW TONGUES) 68
PROPHETIC UTTERANCES IN TONGUES 69
DIFFERENT KINDS OF TONGUES 70
    Some Tongues are for a Sign 73
    Prophesying in Tongues 74
A PERSONAL PRAYER LANGUAGE 75
    The Spirit Helps Us Pray 76
    The Spirit Of Anti-Christ 78
    The Woman Of Revelation, Chapter 12 79
THE GIFTS VS. THE REALITY OF CHRIST....................................80

RESURRECTION **83**

PERFECTION (FULL STATURE)..83
THE RESURRECTION OF CHRIST 84
    The Third Day 86
THE RESURRECTION OF JESUS 88
THE GOSPEL IS NOT SIMPLE 92

BAPTISM INTO CHRIST (FIRE) **95**

SALVATION IS A PROCESS...98
BAPTISM INTO HIS DEATH 101
BAPTISM INTO HIS RESURRECTION 105

The Foolishness of Preaching 105
Spiritual Reproduction 106
The Engrafted Word... 106
Gold and Silver Have I None... 108
The Body Of Christ.. 110
One Spirit... 113
Christ is the Fulfillment of the Law 114
The Race Against Death.. 115
Little Children, Young Men, Fathers................................... 116
One God 118
THE VIEW FROM THE OTHER SIDE 120
Baptism into Satan.. 120

TABLE OF REFERENCES **123**

ABOUT THE AUTHOR **127**

The Alternate Translation Bible©

The Alternate Translation Bible **(ATB)** is an original translation of the Scripture.

Alternate Translation of the Old Testament©
Alternate Translation, Exodus, Chapter 32
    (Crime of the Calf)©
Alternate Translation, Daniel, Chapter 8©
Alternate Translation, Daniel, Chapter 11©

Alternate Translation of the New Testament©
Alternate Translation, 2 Thessalonians, Chapter 2
    (Sophia)©
Alternate Translation, 1st John, Chapter 5©
Alternate Translation, the Book of Colossians
    (To The Church At Colosse) ©
Alternate Translation, the Book of Corinthians, Chapter 11
    (Corinthian Confusion) ©
Alternate Translation, the Book of Jude
    (The Common Salvation)©

Alternate Translation of the Book of the Revelation of Jesus
    Christ to St. John©
Traducción Alternada del Libro de Revelación de Jesucristo©

ALTERNATE TRANSLATIONS IN THIS BOOK

ACTS 10:48 - AT 34

ROM. 7:3 – AT 44

MARK 16:16 – AT: 98

The Truth About Baptism

Baptism

(A Study In Baptism & Tongues)

PROLOGUE

A message from the Lord is for a specific day and time, so you should make every effort to hear it when it is preached. The anointing is on the original word, so even if you hear it later on, it is not the same.

There is a lot of ignorance and pride in the family of God. They pick and choose when and where they go to Church, and do not expect any consequences for their lackadaisical attitude. They ignore the call of the Holy Ghost and are more concerned with their daily activities than their spiritual lives.

We all have responsibilities, but many stay home because they do not feel good, or are tired. Nevertheless, God expects us to come when He calls, or miss what He is doing at that moment.

It saddens me, but I know that God is righteous and I am just a sentimental fool. My heart says, Lord, help them to understand. But He does not, and in the hour that he appears without them, many will ask, how did this happen to me?

He is going to tell them, I called you, and this level of message that I gave at that time would have built such and such a level of Christ in you, and the message that I gave on another occasion would have built that level of Christ in you, but you missed the first two years. You did not submit to enough ministry for Christ to mature enough to bring you to perfection. I did my part. I provided the ministry, but you did not come. There are going to be a lot of really shocked people around.

i

Many do not believe me, but it is true anyhow. You are very blessed that you heard the call of the Lord and are hungry for the Word of God.

Many people out there are jaded. They do not care whether they learn or not. I used to get angry, but I am not angry any more. I am just sad, because there is nothing I can do about it.

The Lord has been letting Christians that follow after their own mind go their own way for many years now. That is the Lord's business, and the reality of the Kingdom. Jesus will call and call, but because judgment does not fall for a long time, people are deceived as to the seriousness of their disobedience.

There were 250,000 people in Central Park to hear a basic salvation message. They bought T-shirts, and popcorn, and made a carnival out of it. I am not saying that it did not do some good. I am emphasizing that, when the call to move on to perfection sounds, very few Christians, compared to the numbers in Central Park, are here.

If you are honest with yourself, that is the reality of the Scripture. Jesus said they would not come when He called them.

Father, I ask that you help me to bring forth this message because, despite all the hours I put in, I really did not have enough time, and my notes are not as I would like them to be. I pray that you help me to bring it forth Lord, that you bless it, and that you open the ears of the hearers. Amen.

INTRODUCTION

The Lord gave me a message on the different types of baptism today, which answers questions that I have been asking for a long time.

For example, a lot of Christians think that if you do not have the Holy Ghost and speak in tongues, you do not have a relationship with Jesus. But I have observed many people, Baptists for example, who have faith in God and a very real relationship with Jesus Christ, but do not speak in tongues. Yet, I see the Lord moving in their lives.

I heard one preacher say that if you have faith in Jesus Christ that is the baptism with the Holy Ghost. A lot of people in denominations that reject speaking in tongues will tell you that they have the Holy Ghost.

The Jehovah's Witnesses say that they have the Holy Ghost. I have been praying about this for years, and now the Lord has shown me that the Scripture speaks about something called the *Baptism with Faith in Jesus Christ.*

The Lord told me several years ago that there is a relationship with God that is based upon the faith of mortal man's carnal mind. I could not find it in the Scripture at that time, but He has shown it to me now.

Sheila R. Vitale

THREE STAGES OF BAPTISM FOR THE CARNAL MIND

(1) Baptism with Water establishes a relationship between the individual and Jesus Christ,

(2) Baptism with the Holy Spirit imparts the power to conceive Christ, who overcomes the carnal mind, and

(3) Baptism with Fire imparts power to the personality to prefer Christ over the carnal mind.

Christ Jesus is the spiritual fire that consumes the sin nature that is holding the personality captive. This baptism is called the ***Baptism into Christ,*** or ***Putting on Christ***.

TWO STAGES OF
HOLY SPIRIT BAPTISM

Baptism with the Holy Spirit comes in two stages,

(1) Receiving the Holy Ghost and

(2) The Baptism with the Holy Ghost.

The apostles, who were baptized with the Holy Spirit on the day of Pentecost and spoke in OTHER TONGUES, had a *measure* of the Holy Spirit that tongue-talking believers in the Church do not have today.

I have been praying about this for a long time. I said, Lord, everybody that I know that has the Holy Spirit speaks in tongues, but I do not hear anybody saying, that is Greek, or that is Russian. We have interpretation of tongues, but that is a spiritual interpretation, not a translation. I have never seen anyone walk into the Church and say, that is Serbian, or whatever their language may be.

COMMENT: My tongues were recognized as Aramaic once.

PASTOR VITALE: Well, praise the Lord, but that is not typical. Did it happen to you once or many times?

COMMENT: Only one time.

PASTOR VITALE: A one-time experience indicates that a special gift came upon you on that one occasion, to accomplish God's specific purpose.

Even if you were to experience speaking in ***other tongues*** all the time, it would still be unusual for today's believers. I do not see the average believer speaking in tongues with other people witnessing that those tongues are a known language.

We are given a ***prayer language*** when we receive the Holy Ghost, and this prayer language type of tongues seems to be the tongues that are prevalent today.

THE CURSE UPON BABEL REVERSED IN THE HOLY SPIRIT

There are two manifestations of Baptism with the Holy Spirit, one greater and one lesser; one with more power and the other with less power. The one with more power was poured out upon the apostles as a witness to men everywhere that the curse of Babel was being reversed.

God cursed mankind at Babel, which resulted in his being divided into many carnal minds, many human bodies, many different nationalities, and many different colors. God also divided him in his thinking and in his language, which produced different cultures.

That is why each of an assortment of ethnic groups can have radically different cultures. You can find yourself in a lot of trouble if you go from one country to another without a revelation of the local customs and, in particular, their view of morality.

Man was divided at the Tower of Babel. He was divided in his flesh through the color of his flesh, and he was divided in his speech, and in his language.

The difference between *speech* and *language* is that one communicates with a particular *spoken language*, such as French, Russian, or English, but *speech* refers to the *thought* that produces the language. You and I can have the same *speech* if we are thinking the same thought, while speaking different *languages*, such as English or French.

Man was divided in *language*, and he was also divided in his *speech* at the Tower of Babel, setting different ethnic groups, one against the other.

What is the witness of that curse in the world today? Countries and individuals all over the world are still waging war and fighting against each other.

The apostles stood up and spoke in the native tongues of men from all over the world, and the men who heard them understood what the apostles were saying in their own language.

This event was an announcement and a witness that the curse of Babel was reversed for everyone who is baptized with the Holy Ghost. Now all men of all nations, languages, speech, and ethnic backgrounds will hear and understand the Word of the Lord when it is spoken.

Yet, there is no witness to this great event in the Church today. We babble a little in some UNKNOWN TONGUES in Church, which are interpreted sometimes, and the local fellowship is edified. But, nothing as glorious as announcing the reversal of the curse of Babel is happening.

UNKNOWN TONGUES, the lesser expression of the Holy Spirit, manifests publicly as tongues which need to be interpreted, and privately as a personal prayer language between the believer and God.

As we said earlier, the greater expression of the Baptism with the Holy Spirit was revealed through the apostles. We will go into more detail about tongues later on.

JESUS ANOINTED

There is one more step beyond the two stages of the Baptism with the Holy Spirit that Jesus experienced, but the apostles did not. Jesus of Nazareth was *anointed* with the Holy Spirit.

Acts 10:38

> [38] HOW **GOD ANOINTED JESUS** OF NAZARETH WITH THE HOLY GHOST AND WITH POWER: . . . . **KJV**

He was not *baptized* with the Holy Spirit.

The word, *anointed*, signifies *oil,* as opposed to *water*. Water flows over and then drains off, but oil leaves a residue, even after it has risen up and subsided.

That is the man, Jesus of Nazareth.

Believers *receive* the Holy Ghost, and the apostles were *filled with* the Holy Ghost, but Jesus was *anointed* with the Holy Ghost. *Anointed* means *to be covered over completely with a sticky substance*.

The Scripture is saying that it is possible to be temporarily filled with the Holy Ghost, which brings you up to full stature . . .

Eph 4:13

> [13] TILL WE ALL COME IN THE UNITY OF THE FAITH, AND OF THE KNOWLEDGE OF THE SON OF GOD, UNTO A

7

PERFECT MAN, UNTO THE MEASURE OF **THE STATURE OF THE FULNESS OF CHRIST**:   **KJV**

. . . and then subsides, if there is something that God wants to do through you.

Jesus Christ of Nazareth was ***anointed*** with the Holy Ghost. The Holy Ghost abided upon Him. The anointing covered Him over and it stuck to Him. It didn't roll off of His back.

Jesus Christ is in the process of anointing us with the Holy Spirit, in the same way that the Father anointed Him, so that Christ Jesus can permanently overlay our carnal mind. Once again, this Scripture is speaking about ***full stature***, or ***perfection***.

So, we see that there is a third stage of the impartation of the Holy Ghost to mankind:

(1) ***Receiving*** the Holy Ghost - Those who received the Holy Ghost spoke in angel's tongues and prophesied.

(2) ***Filled*** with the Holy Ghost - Those who were filled with the Holy Ghost spoke supernaturally in recognizable human languages that they themselves did not know.

(3) ***Anointed*** with the Holy Ghost - Jesus, who was anointed with the Holy Ghost, went about doing good, healing the sick, and casting out devils.

Doing good means that Jesus healed the sick and cast out devils by the power of Christ Jesus. The healing and deliverance in the Church today is done by the carnal mind ***under the control of the Holy Spirit***.

That is why we do not have the same victory that Jesus had in these areas. The Church is only in the first stage, receiving the Holy Ghost, but I think we will start to mature more quickly very soon.

Putting On Christ

The personality ***puts on Christ*** when she prefers Him over the carnal mind, and then ***Christ baptizes the carnal mind*** of that personality (incapacitates her).

Baptism with the Holy Spirit is a level of consciousness, or spirituality. The personality rises into perfection (full stature) by the power of the Holy Ghost ***before*** the individual overcomes his own sin nature, and then returns to its own level of consciousness when the purposes of God have been accomplished. ***Baptism with the Holy Spirit is a condition of temporary perfection***.

JOHN'S BAPTISM FOR THE REMISSION OF SIN

Water Baptism

In **Acts 19:4-6,** Paul said,

Acts 19:4

> [4] . . . JOHN VERILY BAPTIZED WITH THE **BAPTISM OF
> REPENTANCE,** SAYING UNTO THE PEOPLE, THAT THEY
> SHOULD BELIEVE ON HIM WHICH SHOULD COME AFTER HIM,
> THAT IS, ON CHRIST JESUS. **KJV**

Submission to John's Baptism is admission and public renunciation of our sin nature, which is symbolically overshadowed by submerging our physical body under water. *Water Baptism is a symbolic remission, or calling back, of our sin nature.*

Jesus is still saying today, If you confess that you have a sin nature, repent (by faith), and submit to having a man dunk you under the water, I will do in the Spirit (heaven) what you have done in the earth. If you symbolically overcome your sin nature as an act of faith, I will make it a spiritual reality for you. If you go under the physical water as an act of obedience, based upon your belief that I (Jesus) can save you from the domination of your sin nature, I will immerse that sin nature in the Spirit of Christ (Lake of Fire) and dissolve it.

11

So, we see that FALLEN MAN'S FAITH in God provides forgiveness to the man who is living out of his sin nature BY FAITH, but not in reality, because he still sins.

We know that our forgiveness is not in reality because, if we are honest with ourselves, we sin every day. It is THE FAITH OF THE SON OF GOD, which is Christ, the manchild formed in the individual, that gives us the hope of deliverance from the tyranny of our sin nature (carnal mind), and of glorification.

Some are preaching against water baptism today, which is a big mistake. This same spirit is operating in preachers and believers alike, who have been in deliverance ministry for years. Preaching against deliverance for young Christians, after having received the benefits of deliverance ministry for oneself, can be likened to a college graduate saying that high school is no longer necessary.

The most positive statement I can make about this line of thought is that it is the fruit of ignorance. It is not rational to expect believers to mature spiritually when they are deprived of a foundational ministry that you, yourself, have benefitted from. These same preachers that deny deliverance then tell the people crying out for help that they are not healed because they lack faith. This is much more than ignorance. It is wickedness against those who Jesus died for.

My response to the wave of preaching against water baptism today, is this: No one is willing to acknowledge more than I that water baptism is an act of the flesh, but it is the act by which carnal people can enter into a spiritual contract with the Lord Jesus Christ. They are not spiritual. There is nothing spiritual about them, but the Lord Jesus has made a way for them to become spiritual through a relationship with Him.

It is like telling a two-year-old to put his own clothes on, and then helping him just enough so that he can say that he put his own jacket on. That is what water baptism is. The Lord Jesus is saying,

Just show this much of an interest in Me, show Me that you want Me just that little bit, and I will do the whole thing in reality.

It is a big mistake to tell youngsters in Christ not to obey this commandment of God. Water baptism, even though it is a work of the flesh, is a covenant that Jesus Christ made with humanity that is still in full force and effect. The Lord Jesus is still honoring it.

Jesus' covenant of water baptism will fade away when every human being on the face of the earth has either experienced it, or is spiritually mature enough to not need it. It is wrong to disannul it because you have experienced it, but do not need it any more. Water baptism is a beautiful spiritual experience for anyone who has just come to Christ. Do not take it away from the babies.

Christ vs. Christ Jesus

In *Acts 19:4-6*, Paul said, *John verily baptized with the Baptism of Repentance*. John told the people *to believe on* Christ Jesus, the one who should come after John the Baptist, who was doing the work of the flesh.

John did not tell them that they should believe on *Jesus of Nazareth*. He said that they should believe on *Christ Jesus*. Christ Jesus is the Christ resurrected in an individual, married to the Lord Jesus, who is above.

The resurrected Adam in a mortal man is called *Christ*. *Christ* is mortal man's new, righteous mind. Adam rose from the dead in Jesus of Nazareth and dominated His carnal mind. After that, Jesus of Nazareth became Jesus, the Christ.

Had Jesus been as selfish as the rest of the human race, He would have said, *I went through it, I overcame, I did it, I'm perfected and that is the end of it, I am not doing anything else.* But Jesus did not stop there. He said, *If a corn of wheat falls into the ground it shall bring forth a great harvest.*

Jesus, the Christ, and the Father are one. This means that the Father's Spirit joined with the resurrected Adam, Jesus' righteous mind (called Christ Jesus in the New Testament). The Father and Jesus had a spiritual marriage, and, so, Jesus, the Christ, became Christ Jesus after His righteous mind married the Father, who is above.

After that, Christ Jesus, Jesus' new inner man, who is in the image of God . . . .

Col 3:10

> [10] AND HAVE PUT ON **THE NEW MAN**, WHICH IS RENEWED IN KNOWLEDGE AFTER THE IMAGE OF HIM THAT CREATED HIM: **KJV**

. . . . gave up His flesh existence to become a magnificent spiritual man. Today, Christ Jesus is raining His virile seed upon mortal man . . .

1 Peter 1:2

> [2] ELECT ACCORDING TO THE FOREKNOWLEDGE OF GOD THE FATHER, THROUGH SANCTIFICATION OF THE SPIRIT, UNTO OBEDIENCE AND SPRINKLING OF THE BLOOD OF JESUS CHRIST: GRACE UNTO YOU, AND PEACE, BE MULTIPLIED.
> **KJV**

. . . to beget the children that the Father promised Him: The second generation of Christ.

1 Tim 2:5

⁵ FOR THERE IS ONE GOD, AND ONE MEDIATOR
BETWEEN GOD AND MEN, **THE MAN CHRIST JESUS**; **KJV**

Col 3:10

¹⁰ AND HAVE PUT ON **THE NEW MAN**, WHICH IS
RENEWED IN KNOWLEDGE AFTER THE IMAGE OF HIM THAT
CREATED HIM: **KJV**

1 Peter 1:2

² ELECT ACCORDING TO THE FOREKNOWLEDGE OF
GOD THE FATHER, THROUGH SANCTIFICATION OF THE
SPIRIT, UNTO OBEDIENCE AND SPRINKLING OF THE BLOOD OF
JESUS CHRIST: GRACE UNTO YOU, AND PEACE, **BE
MULTIPLIED. KJV**

That is, Christ in you, and in me -- the second generation of
Christ, which is about to have a similar experience. The Lord
Jesus, who is now above, is marrying the resurrected Christ in
each of us, which gives us the strength to overcome our carnal
mind.

We see in the book of Acts that John not only baptized in water,
but he counseled the people, saying, *It is not enough to be
dunked under the water, you must believe on the One that is to
come, even Christ Jesus.* We must believe on the second
generation of Christ.

As your physical body goes down under the water, believe that
there is a second generation of Christ -- that Adam will rise from
the dead in you also.

The Gospel of the Cross vs. The Gospel of Perfection

When John said, ***Believe on Christ Jesus***, he was counseling the people to believe the Gospel of Perfection, not the Gospel of the Cross.

The Gospel of the Cross is the account of Jesus of Nazareth's personal experience. But John was not talking about God being in the midst of the man, Jesus of Nazareth. He was talking to the one being baptized, saying, ***Believe that Christ will rise from the dead in you also, and that the resurrected Christ within you will marry the Father, Who is above.***

John was talking about ***the Gospel of Perfection***. He was talking about the resurrection of the dead. He was preaching about the second generation of the resurrected Adam, Elohim's Son . . .

Luke 3:38

> [38] WHICH WAS THE SON OF ENOS, WHICH WAS THE SON OF SETH, WHICH WAS THE SON OF ADAM, WHICH WAS **THE SON OF GOD. KJV**

. . . .who was to be conceived, nurtured and brought to term by the first generation of Christ, the Lord Jesus.

Luke 3:38

> [38] WHICH WAS THE SON OF ENOS, WHICH WAS THE SON OF SETH, WHICH WAS THE SON OF ADAM, WHICH WAS **THE SON OF GOD. KJV**

COMMENT: Every time you hear ***Christ Jesus,*** does it mean the second generation?

PASTOR VITALE: No, it does not.

Jesus is the personality whose carnal mind was overshadowed by (baptized into) Christ, when He preferred *Christ* over his carnal mind. After that, Jesus, the Christ, was glorified and became Savior of the world.

Christ is the resurrected Adam, our only hope of being glorified.

Christ Jesus is the resurrected Adam, married to the Father who is above, appearing in any personality.

A Call to Repentance

<u>Matt 3:11</u>

> [11] I INDEED **BAPTIZE YOU WITH WATER UNTO REPENTANCE**: BUT HE THAT COMETH AFTER ME IS MIGHTIER THAN I, WHOSE SHOES I AM NOT WORTHY TO BEAR: HE SHALL BAPTIZE YOU WITH THE HOLY GHOST, AND WITH FIRE: **KJV**

John rebuked the Pharisees and the Sadducees who came to his Baptism, saying, *Oh generation of vipers, who hath warned you to flee from the wrath to come*, meaning, you want water baptism so that your sins will be remitted, but without confession and repentance. You have no idea what you are asking for.

Going under the water is only your part of the contract that water baptism establishes between you and God. God's promise in this contract is to submerge your carnal mind under Christ, who is the Lake of Fire.

John called the Pharisees a generation of vipers, saying, *Count the cost, do not take this water baptism lightly, because the fiery processing that comes from God's side of the contract will destroy your carnal mind. You can see water baptism, but you cannot see the burning, fiery, righteous judgment of your sin nature that follows. You can only survive it if Christ is in you.*

John was saying, *Check yourself out. There is a potential for salvation in you, but we know that all Israel is not Israel,*

Rom 9:6

> [6] NOT AS THOUGH THE WORD OF GOD HATH TAKEN NONE EFFECT. FOR **THEY ARE NOT ALL ISRAEL**, WHICH ARE OF ISRAEL: **KJV**

Jesus said*, there are four kinds of soil* (Mk 13:4-8)*, but only one of them is good soil.*

Matt 13:8

> [8] BUT OTHER FELL INTO GOOD GROUND, AND **BROUGHT FORTH FRUIT**, SOME AN HUNDREDFOLD, SOME SIXTYFOLD, SOME THIRTYFOLD. **KJV**

Check yourself out, because this is no game. Fire from heaven is coming down upon you after I dunk you under this water, so you had better leave now if you are fooling around.

John goes on to say:

Matt 3:11-12

> [11] ... HE SHALL BAPTIZE YOU WITH THE HOLY GHOST, AND WITH FIRE:
>
> [12] WHOSE FAN IS IN HIS HAND, AND HE WILL THROUGHLY PURGE HIS FLOOR, AND GATHER HIS WHEAT INTO THE GARNER; BUT **HE WILL BURN UP THE CHAFF WITH UNQUENCHABLE FIRE. KJV**

The faithful who were coming to be baptized in water for the remission of sins did not need to hear this. John was warning the ungodly, ***Do not play with God.***

Many Christians desire knowledge of the deep teachings of God because they want to glorify themselves by teaching others. But the Holy Ghost reveals their true motives and, when they will not repent, they go under judgment. I have seen it happen.

You cannot capture the Anointing. The deeper the ministry you are trying to use for your own purposes, the more dangerous your indiscretion is. We reap what we sow, brethren, and those who try to capture the Anointing, will suffer the loss of the Anointing.

Baptism with the Holy Ghost means to be under the total control of the Holy Ghost.

Most who are speaking in tongues today are ***EXPERIENCING*** the Holy Ghost, some when they are in Church, and others when they are at home, but very few, if any, are under its complete control.

Most believers live out of their sin nature, even at Church, because they are under the influence of the Holy Ghost, not filled up with it.

We have just looked at two Scriptures that speak about the ***Baptism with the Holy Ghost.*** The one we just talked about, which promises the Holy Ghost to the Sadducees and Pharisees, even those in the Church today, has no time limit on it. But John said to the apostles, ***In a few days*** . . . . John did not say next year you are going to be baptized with the Holy Ghost. John said to the apostles, ***The Lord said***, ***in a few days you will be baptized with the Holy Ghost***. John was talking about the outpouring at Pentecost:

Acts 2:2

> **2** AND SUDDENLY THERE CAME **A SOUND FROM
> HEAVEN AS OF A RUSHING MIGHTY WIND**, AND IT FILLED
> ALL THE HOUSE WHERE THEY WERE SITTING. **KJV**

I used to read this Scripture and think that the Sadducees and the
Pharisees went away. But, as I read it today, I see that the
Scripture is not clear about whether they turned away, or they
repented. My guess is that some turned away and some repented.

The following is a parallel account of John the Baptist, this time
addressing the multitude.

Luke 3:7-15

> **7** THEN **SAID HE TO THE MULTITUDE** THAT CAME
> FORTH TO BE BAPTIZED OF HIM, O GENERATION OF VIPERS,
> WHO HATH WARNED YOU TO FLEE FROM THE WRATH TO
> COME?

Apparently, as is true today, the faithful were very few, so John
spoke to the multitude.

> **8** **BRING FORTH THEREFORE FRUITS WORTHY OF
> REPENTANCE**, AND BEGIN NOT TO SAY WITHIN YOURSELVES,
> WE HAVE ABRAHAM TO OUR FATHER: FOR I SAY UNTO YOU,
> THAT GOD IS ABLE OF THESE STONES TO RAISE UP CHILDREN
> UNTO ABRAHAM.
>
> **9** AND NOW ALSO THE AXE IS LAID UNTO THE ROOT
> OF THE TREES: EVERY TREE THEREFORE WHICH BRINGETH
> NOT FORTH GOOD FRUIT IS HEWN DOWN, AND CAST INTO THE
> FIRE.
>
> **10** AND THE PEOPLE ASKED HIM, SAYING, WHAT
> SHALL WE DO THEN?
>
> **11** HE ANSWERETH AND SAITH UNTO THEM, HE
> THAT HATH TWO COATS, LET HIM IMPART TO HIM THAT HATH
> NONE; AND HE THAT HATH MEAT, LET HIM DO LIKEWISE.

¹² THEN CAME ALSO PUBLICANS TO BE BAPTIZED,
AND SAID UNTO HIM, MASTER, WHAT SHALL WE DO?

¹³ AND HE SAID UNTO THEM, EXACT NO MORE THAN
THAT WHICH IS APPOINTED YOU.

¹⁴ AND THE SOLDIERS LIKEWISE DEMANDED OF HIM,
SAYING, AND WHAT SHALL WE DO? AND HE SAID UNTO
THEM, DO VIOLENCE TO NO MAN, NEITHER ACCUSE ANY
FALSELY; AND BE CONTENT WITH YOUR WAGES.

¹⁵ AND AS THE PEOPLE WERE IN EXPECTATION, AND
ALL MEN MUSED IN THEIR HEARTS OF JOHN, WHETHER HE
WERE THE CHRIST, OR NOT; **KJV**

Verses 7-15 indicate that the multitude said to John, ***What shall
we do?*** John's answer was, ***Repent AND CHANGE YOUR
WAYS***.

John meant, repent by faith and then repent in reality by changing
your ways. Saying that you should repent is not enough. You
have to change your behavior and start acting like Christ. Resist
the ungodly thoughts of your carnal mind, and Christ will
overthrow those thoughts and give you peace.

<u>James 4:7</u>

⁷ SUBMIT YOURSELVES THEREFORE TO GOD.
RESIST THE DEVIL, AND HE WILL FLEE FROM YOU. **KJV**

21

SPIRITUAL BAPTISM

So, we see that the first baptism, water, leads to the second baptism, Spirit. But, actually, there is just one baptism. The Scripture says there is one faith and one baptism, and whole denominations draw the conclusion that it is the baptism with water. But this is not true.

The one baptism is a spiritual baptism which we ascend into by stages. We are not *descending* into spiritual baptism. Christ Jesus is descending *upon us*, as we rise to meet Him

2 Cor 5:2,4

> [2] FOR IN THIS WE GROAN, EARNESTLY **DESIRING TO BE CLOTHED UPON** WITH OUR HOUSE WHICH IS FROM HEAVEN:

> [4] FOR WE THAT ARE IN THIS TABERNACLE DO GROAN, BEING BURDENED: NOT FOR THAT WE WOULD BE UNCLOTHED, BUT **CLOTHED UPON**, THAT MORTALITY MIGHT BE SWALLOWED UP OF LIFE. **KJV**

COMMENT: A friend of mine was furious when I told her I was to be baptized in water because my denomination gave that Scripture. I was not grown up enough in the Lord yet, so I gave in, but the Lord told me to be baptized in water later on.

PASTOR VITALE: Oh, you did not get baptized at that time?

COMMENT: No, I felt I was in error.

PASTOR VITALE: What did she say the one baptism was?

23

COMMENT: She said one baptism was enough, and she was screaming at me.

PASTOR VITALE: What was the one baptism to her, the Baptism with the Holy Spirit?

COMMENT: No, not even that. The baby . . . .

PASTOR VITALE: Oh, the sprinkling.

COMMENT: I repented.

PASTOR VITALE: Well, praise the Lord that He brought you to the truth.

A little research will reveal that there are many baptisms. There is a baptism with fire, a baptism of suffering, etc., but there is really only one baptism in many parts. There is one body, many members thereof; one Godhead, different expressions thereof; one Spirit, many administrations. There is only one baptism with many stages.

As Christ increases in us, the personality, which we are, continues to be baptized deeper and deeper into Christ Jesus' spiritual life.

The first step is to have someone dunk you under the water, which is an act of faith. Our powerful and glorious Savior, the Lord Jesus Christ, is saying, ***Go into the water of your own free will, and I will carry you the rest of the way.*** As far as I am concerned, that makes water baptism a very, very, important act of faith.

The second stage of baptism, spiritual baptism, is revealed as the first stage of baptism, water baptism, takes place. Submission to the first baptism, immersion in water, which is an act of ***mortal man's faith***, leads to the beginning stage of the second baptism, the spiritual baptism that imparts the ***faith of the Son of God*** to the believer.

24

Gal 2:20

> [20] I AM CRUCIFIED WITH CHRIST: NEVERTHELESS I LIVE; YET NOT I, BUT CHRIST LIVETH IN ME: AND THE LIFE WHICH I NOW LIVE IN THE FLESH *I LIVE BY THE FAITH OF THE SON OF GOD*, WHO LOVED ME, AND GAVE HIMSELF FOR ME. **KJV**

Mortal man can believe the Gospel of the Cross, but only the *faith of the Son of God*, Christ in us . . .

Col 1:27

> [27] TO WHOM GOD WOULD MAKE KNOWN WHAT IS THE RICHES OF THE GLORY OF THIS MYSTERY AMONG THE GENTILES; WHICH IS **CHRIST IN YOU, THE HOPE OF GLORY**: **KJV**

. . . can believe God's true plan of salvation for the human race. Our carnal mind cannot believe, so Christ in us believes for us. Our carnal mind cannot understand, so Christ in us becomes our understanding.

Water baptism is an act of mortal faith which prepares the heart to receive the engrafted Word and the Spirit of Truth. The Holy Spirit, the Spirit of the Father, joins with our human spirit. This is the first stage of our spiritual marriage. Eventually, we conceive the engrafted Word, the manchild, even Christ, who is our faith.

Baptism – An Act of faith

It is not enough to have faith *in* Jesus, the Christ. We must have the faith *of* Christ Jesus, which is the resurrected Adam.

25

It is impossible for your carnal mind to have the faith of Christ Jesus. Adam is the Son of God, and the mortal that he rises from the dead in, becomes a Son of God.

The second generation of Christ (the Church), are Sons of God because the Lord Jesus has impregnated us with Himself, enabling Adam to rise from the dead in us also. The Lord Jesus, the first generation of Christ, together with His children, the second generation of Christ, are the many-membered Sons of God. But Jesus is the Head of His body.

Col 1:18

> [18] AND **HE IS THE HEAD OF THE BODY,** THE CHURCH: WHO IS THE BEGINNING, THE FIRSTBORN FROM THE DEAD; THAT IN ALL THINGS HE MIGHT HAVE THE PREEMINENCE. **KJV**

There is only one way that we can have the faith of Jesus Christ, and that is to bear His child. Salvation, faith and understanding are in Christ, the manchild. We must conceive and bear the manchild, because He is our life. The barren shall surely continue to die, so, if you are not pregnant with Christ, ask the Lord Jesus to impregnate you.

BAPTISM IN THE NAME OF THE LORD JESUS

Paul preaches the ***Gospel of Perfection*** to the disciples at Ephesus and baptizes those who understand it into the ***Name*** of, or the ***Spirit*** of, the Lord Jesus Christ.

Acts 19:4

> [4] THEN SAID PAUL, JOHN VERILY BAPTIZED WITH THE BAPTISM OF REPENTANCE, SAYING UNTO THE PEOPLE, THAT THEY SHOULD **BELIEVE ON HIM WHICH SHOULD COME AFTER HIM, THAT IS, ON CHRIST JESUS.** KJV

When they heard John say, ***Believe in the one who comes after me*** . . .

Acts 19:5

> [5] WHEN THEY HEARD THIS, **THEY WERE BAPTIZED IN THE NAME OF THE LORD JESUS.** KJV

. . . they were baptized in the ***Name*** of the Lord Jesus Christ.

Paul must have said a lot more than the short verse quoted here. He must have preached the whole ***Gospel of Perfection*** to them, and when they heard it, ***They were baptized in the Name***, or ***Spirit, of the Lord Jesus Christ***.

When I was a young Christian, I was water baptized in the name of the Father, the Son, and the Holy Ghost. About one year later there was a big flurry in our local fellowship. A couple of

27

preachers came in saying that the apostles baptized in the Name of *Jesus*, so we had better be baptized again. But there is only one water Baptism, John's Baptism, and that is unto repentance. It does not matter whether you are baptized in the Name of Jesus, or the Father, the Son and the Holy Ghost, as long as you have repented of known sin.

The Gospel of the Cross vs.
The Gospel of the Kingdom

The Baptism in the Name of the Lord Jesus is the impartation of faith through the preaching of the Kingdom of God.

The man who hears the *Gospel of the Cross* preached by the carnal mind is baptized (fully immersed) into the spirit of the preacher, and the hearer's carnal mind may, or may not, believe that Jesus Christ is the Savior of his soul (personality).

Unfortunately, more often than not, the message accompanying the Gospel of the Cross says that we are being saved from a burning hell, which is not the message of the Scripture.

The man who hears the *Gospel of the Kingdom* preached by Christ Jesus and is baptized (fully immersed) into the spirit of the preacher . . .

1 Cor 10:2

> [2] AND WERE **ALL BAPTIZED UNTO MOSES** IN THE CLOUD AND IN THE SEA; **KJV**

. . . receives the virile seed which raises Christ from the dead in that man. But, not everyone who hears is baptized and conceives Christ.

Luke 8:5-8

> [5] A SOWER WENT OUT TO SOW HIS SEED: AND AS HE SOWED, **SOME FELL BY THE WAY SIDE**; AND IT WAS TRODDEN DOWN, AND THE FOWLS OF THE AIR DEVOURED IT.
>
> [6] AND **SOME FELL UPON A ROCK**; AND AS SOON AS IT WAS SPRUNG UP, IT WITHERED AWAY, BECAUSE IT LACKED MOISTURE.
>
> [7] AND **SOME FELL AMONG THORNS**; AND THE THORNS SPRANG UP WITH IT, AND CHOKED IT.
>
> [8] AND OTHER **FELL ON GOOD GROUND**, AND SPRANG UP, AND BARE FRUIT AN HUNDREDFOLD. AND WHEN HE HAD SAID THESE THINGS, HE CRIED, HE THAT HATH EARS TO HEAR, LET HIM HEAR. **KJV**

There is only one physical baptism, and that is water baptism. After that, we move into spiritual baptism which has several stages.

You can dunk someone's head under water 1,500 times saying, *in the Name of the Father, the Name of the Son, the Name of the Holy Ghost, in the Name of Jesus, in the name of fire*, but these are just vain words arising out of your carnal mind. Something spiritual has to happen to you, or the baptism is of no effect.

The Church has to get out of the letter and start moving in the spiritual understanding of the Scripture. This is no game. If you do not have this spiritual baby, you will continue to die. Unfortunately, most Christians believe their soul is delivered *after* the death of their physical body, which is a lie, and ignore the signs of death closing in on them.

Again, verse 5 says, ***And when they heard the gospel of the Kingdom, they were baptized in the Name of the Lord Jesus***.

Acts 19:5

> [5] WHEN THEY HEARD THIS, **THEY WERE BAPTIZED IN THE NAME OF THE LORD JESUS. KJV**

Christ Jesus in Paul was mature enough to impart virile seed to these believers through the foolishness of preaching. The Word Paul preached baptized them with the Name, or Nature, of the Lord Jesus Christ, and they received the seed.

Then, verse 6 says, After they were baptized in the Name of the Lord Jesus, ***Paul laid hands upon them and the Holy Ghost came upon them, and they spoke with tongues and prophesied***.

Acts 19:6

> [6] AND WHEN PAUL HAD LAID HIS HANDS UPON THEM, **THE HOLY GHOST CAME ON THEM**; AND THEY SPAKE WITH TONGUES, AND PROPHESIED. **KJV**

Cornelius and his house believed Peter's message also, and they were baptized in the Name of the Lord Jesus and received the Holy Ghost.

Acts 10:44

> [44] WHILE PETER YET SPAKE THESE WORDS, **THE HOLY GHOST FELL ON ALL THEM WHICH HEARD THE WORD**. KJV

Now remember, Paul did not preach the ***Gospel of the Cross***, that Jesus is Savior. He preached the ***Gospel of the Kingdom***, the resurrection and formation of Christ in the individual.

Gal 4:19

¹⁹ MY LITTLE CHILDREN, OF WHOM I TRAVAIL IN BIRTH AGAIN **UNTIL CHRIST BE FORMED IN YOU,** **KJV**

Those who are baptized with the lesser expression of the ***Baptism in the Name of the Lord Jesus*** believe that Christ can be resurrected in them, and receive the Holy Ghost; and those who are baptized with the greater expression of the ***Baptism in the Name of the Lord Jesus*** receive the virile seed of Christ, the engrafted Word.

James 1:21

²¹ WHEREFORE LAY APART ALL FILTHINESS AND SUPERFLUITY OF NAUGHTINESS, AND **RECEIVE WITH MEEKNESS THE ENGRAFTED WORD, WHICH IS ABLE TO SAVE YOUR SOULS.** **KJV**

Receiving the Holy Ghost

Cornelius was open to any spiritual experience that the Lord would give him, and he received the Holy Ghost. As far as I know, with very few exceptions, everyone who believes that Jesus is the Son of God and Savior, and wants the Holy Ghost, receives it.

Those who do not receive the Holy Ghost usually do not want it, because they believe that the Holy Ghost in the Church today is not of God.

The whole purpose of water baptism is to give the Jew an opportunity to humble himself before God through confession of sin. I say ***confession*** rather than ***repentance***, because true repentance is rejection of the carnal mind in favor of the Christ mind. This is only possible if Christ, our new mind, is formed in us. John knew this and the Jews understood it also.

Acts 10:2 says, ***Cornelius was,***

Acts 10:2,4

> [2] **A DEVOUT MAN**, AND ONE THAT FEARED GOD WITH ALL HIS HOUSE, WHICH GAVE MUCH ALMS TO THE PEOPLE, AND PRAYED TO GOD ALWAY.
>
> [3] HE SAW IN A VISION EVIDENTLY ABOUT THE NINTH HOUR OF THE DAY **AN ANGEL OF GOD COMING IN TO HIM**, AND SAYING UNTO HIM, CORNELIUS.
>
> [4] AND WHEN HE LOOKED ON HIM, HE WAS AFRAID, AND SAID, WHAT IS IT, LORD? AND HE SAID UNTO HIM, THY PRAYERS AND THINE ALMS ARE COME UP FOR A MEMORIAL BEFORE GOD. **KJV**

Cornelius did not need a special occasion to humble himself before God, but the Jews of Jesus' day thought their sins were covered because they kept the law.

Likewise, many Christians today think that their sin nature is covered because they believe that Jesus is Savior, or that Christ covers their sin nature without first exposing and defeating it.

Cornelius' humility before the God of the Jews moved Christ towards him, and Cornelius' obedience to Christ (the Angel who spoke to him) sent Peter to preach the ***Gospel of the Cross to him***.

Acts 10:30-31

> [30] AND CORNELIUS SAID, FOUR DAYS AGO I WAS FASTING UNTIL THIS HOUR; AND AT THE NINTH HOUR I PRAYED IN MY HOUSE, AND, **BEHOLD, A MAN STOOD BEFORE ME IN BRIGHT CLOTHING,**

> ³¹ AND SAID, CORNELIUS, THY PRAYER IS HEARD,
> AND THINE ALMS ARE HAD IN REMEMBRANCE IN THE SIGHT
> OF GOD. **KJV**

When Cornelius and his band heard about Jesus' experience, they must have realized that the Angel who appeared to Cornelius was Christ Jesus, the resurrected Adam. They must have also received a supernatural understanding of the *Gospel of the Kingdom* (that Christ can be formed in non-Jews also), because they received the Holy Ghost.

The Virile Seed Of The Lord Jesus

Then Peter, perceiving what happened, commanded that Cornelius and his band should receive the virile seed of Christ, the engrafted Word, the greater expression of the *Baptism in the Name of the Lord Jesus*.

Acts 10:47

> ⁴⁸ AND **HE COMMANDED THEM TO BE BAPTIZED IN THE NAME OF THE LORD**. THEN PRAYED THEY HIM TO TARRY CERTAIN DAYS. **KJV**

I am sorry to disappoint all of you who think that Peter commanded Cornelius to be water baptized . . .

Acts 10:48

> ⁴⁷ CAN ANY MAN FORBID WATER, THAT THESE SHOULD NOT BE BAPTIZED, **WHICH HAVE RECEIVED THE HOLY GHOST AS WELL AS WE**? **KJV**

. . . but the Greek Interlinear text reveals that Peter said,

> *Acts 10:48 - AT*: ***Satan, the*** [spiritual] ***water, could have stopped these men from being baptized, but they have received the Holy Ghost as well as we***, [wherefore, they should be baptized in the Name of the Lord Jesus, as well] (**ATB**)

Of course, to receive this translation, one must have a revelation that **Satan** is the spiritual water upon which the image of this world is appearing, and that any negative particle (in this case, the word, ***not***) can be translated, ***Satan***.

Peter was saying that the Holy Ghost was evidence that Cornelius and his band were eligible to have Christ formed in them. Satan's failure to prevent them from receiving the Holy Spirit was proof that Cornelius and his band had confessed their sins and repented.

Apparently, Christ was already raised ***by faith*** in Cornelius, as He was in many of the Jews, but Christ raised by faith has no root. The Holy Spirit, on the other hand, grafts to the human spirit and raises Christ ***from seed***.

Now, since the personality is saved when it fuses with, or is adopted by, the ***engrafted*** Christ, it is self-evident that a personality fusing to Christ who has been raised by faith (not by seed), has no enduring foundation (root) within himself.

1 Cor 3:11

¹¹ FOR OTHER FOUNDATION CAN NO MAN LAY
THAN THAT IS LAID, WHICH IS JESUS CHRIST. **KJV**

People can speak in tongues without water baptism when God receives the sacrifice of their humility. But be careful that you are not fostering rebellion or arrogance towards God, your pastor, or your local fellowship by thinking that you do not need water baptism.

I was water baptized after I received the Holy Spirit. I was desperate enough to do anything that might bring God's mercy down upon me and my family.

So we see that the ideal order is: Water baptism, faith that Christ will rise from the dead in us, receiving the Holy Ghost (with the witness of speaking in new tongues), and receiving the engrafted Word. But we do not always experience the promises of the New Testament in that order. I spoke in tongues before I was water baptized.

Many in the Church today have faith that Jesus is Savior, have been water baptized and have a relationship with the Holy Spirit, but do not understand about the engrafted Word and the adoption of their personality.

You have to be baptized in the Name of the Lord Jesus Christ, and that does not mean having your head dunked under the water by someone saying, *In the Name of the Lord Jesus*.

The Baptism in the Name of the Lord Jesus is the engrafting of the Lord Jesus' virile seed to your human spirit, and you can only get it from someone who has Jesus' virile seed.

If you have the Holy Ghost because a man laid hands on you, but the Lord Jesus' virile seed has not grafted to your human spirit, it is probably because you have not heard, or believed, the Gospel of the Kingdom.

The sign of your spiritual fertility is the hope that Christ will be formed in you. But if you have not heard the message, you cannot have the hope, and without hope, there can be no faith, because Christ is our faith.

Phil 3:9

[9] AND BE FOUND IN HIM, NOT HAVING MINE OWN RIGHTEOUSNESS, WHICH IS OF THE LAW, BUT **THAT WHICH**

IS THROUGH THE FAITH OF CHRIST, THE RIGHTEOUSNESS
WHICH IS OF GOD BY FAITH: **KJV**

When you plant a vegetable seed in your garden, it takes quite a while before that seed produces a mature plant with its own seed. This too, is true of Christians. Everyone who has received the Lord Jesus' virile seed does not have virile seed to give out. Even if you find someone who has virile seed, the Lord Jesus must be willing to impregnate you.

Sitting in a meeting will not impart Christ to you. Jesus is in control of everything. Many rebels in the Church think they are in control, but they are not. Jesus' virile seed will only engraft to those who have a contrite heart and a broken spirit. That is why James says, ***Receive with meekness the engrafted Word, which is able to save your souls.***

QUESTION: What percentage of people are baptized in the Name of Jesus?

PASTOR VITALE: Quite a few.

Jesus said,

John 4:35

> [35] SAY NOT YE, THERE ARE YET FOUR MONTHS, AND THEN COMETH HARVEST? BEHOLD, I SAY UNTO YOU, LIFT UP YOUR EYES, AND **LOOK ON THE FIELDS; FOR THEY ARE WHITE ALREADY TO HARVEST. KJV**

Contrary to the opinion of many in the Church today, Christ is the one being harvested, or cut away from the carnal mind (sin nature), so that He can ascend above and overshadow it. This spiritually elevated condition is called ***perfection,*** or ***full stature***.

Jesus said,

Luke 10:2

> [2] . . . THE HARVEST TRULY IS GREAT, BUT THE
> LABOURERS ARE FEW: **PRAY YE THEREFORE THE LORD OF**
> **THE HARVEST, THAT HE WOULD SEND FORTH LABOURERS**
> **INTO HIS HARVEST. KJV**

He meant, Pray that the many who have received the baptism in
the Name of the Lord Jesus (the engrafted Word) will wage
spiritual warfare against their own carnal mind, to separate
(harvest) their Christ Mind from the false vine.

Ascension Above The Sin Nature

By and large, the Church world rejects the *Gospel of Perfection*,
the good news that mortal man can ascend above his sin nature
and enter into everlasting life.

Mature believers who expect Christ to appear in mortal man are
shocked to hear that the *Gospel of Perfection* is a part of, and
cannot be separated from, the *Doctrine of Christ* (the spiritual
understanding of the Scripture). I am talking about brethren who
know that the *rapture* is not physical, but the spiritual ascension
of the individual believer.

To the best of my knowledge, most of the brethren who assent to
the *Doctrine of Sonship* (the belief that mortal man can become
a Son of God) also believe in a literal, endless hell, known as
eternal damnation.

The truth is that *this present world*, which is a mixture of good
and evil, *is the hell that the creation fell into* after Adam
submitted to his own evil self, instead of Jehovah. This world had

a beginning, and it will come to an end. God does not punish people forever and ever. He is a giver of Life.

Many in the Sonship camp prefer the doctrine of *eternal damnation* over the truth that *eternal judgment* is Christ Jesus' everlasting restraints upon our carnal mind. This principle is expressed in the New Testament as *the laying on of hands*, or the overlaying by the Mind of Christ.

Heb 6:2

[2] OF THE DOCTRINE OF BAPTISMS, AND OF **LAYING ON OF HANDS,** AND OF RESURRECTION OF THE DEAD, AND OF ETERNAL JUDGMENT. **KJV**

Ultimate Reconciliation

Some assent to the *Doctrine of Ultimate Reconciliation*, which teaches that:

- Adam never fell,

- Mankind is NOT dominated by the inherited sin nature which supplanted Adam, their righteous mind,

- God is responsible for mankind's weak spiritual condition, because He made us this way, and

- God is the author of all negative experiences, which He has ordained for the purpose of maturing mankind,

THEREFORE,

Every personality and physical body which has ever appeared in the earth will be resurrected,

WHEN

Christ in the individual overcomes humanity's spiritual immaturities, and the whole man enters into *perfection*,

WHICH EVENT WILL OCCUR

Without exposing and destroying their lower (sin) nature,

BECAUSE

God deliberately built weakness into His creation, so that He could mature us through overcoming experiences.

But this is not true. Our human spirit is alive through union with the Spirit of Christ . . .

Rom 8:11

> [11] BUT IF **THE SPIRIT OF HIM THAT RAISED UP JESUS FROM THE DEAD** DWELL IN YOU, HE THAT RAISED UP CHRIST FROM THE DEAD SHALL ALSO QUICKEN YOUR MORTAL BODIES BY HIS SPIRIT THAT DWELLETH IN YOU. **KJV**

. . . but our personality (soul) is dead, because of our inherited sin nature.

God is the God of the living. He is the God of the spirit of man. Our personality (soul) and physical body are given to us for the limited season of this present existence.

The human spirit will continue to return to the Father in an endless cycle of births and deaths, until Christ in the individual is quickened, made alive, raised from the dead, through union with the Spirit of Christ; and the physical bodies of this world will continue to die until Christ matures to the degree that He can sustain the life of the personality and physical body that He is living in.

1 Cor 6:17

> [17] BUT HE THAT IS **JOINED UNTO THE LORD** IS ONE SPIRIT. **KJV**

I have heard it preached that we should be nice to our lower (sin) nature because she has been through enough. But I say to you, Do not be nice to your carnal mind, but destroy her before she kills Christ, if He has been raised in you.

Many will continue to believe that they are preaching the true Gospel of God until they experience the **resurrection of the unjust** (spiritual union with the Dragon instead of the Lord Jesus, who is above).

Rev 12:4

> [4] AND HIS TAIL DREW THE THIRD PART OF THE STARS OF HEAVEN, AND DID CAST THEM TO THE EARTH: AND **THE DRAGON STOOD BEFORE THE WOMAN WHICH WAS READY TO BE DELIVERED,** FOR TO DEVOUR HER CHILD AS SOON AS IT WAS BORN. **KJV**

Reconciled to the Lord Jesus

I told you earlier that there are two levels of the **baptism with the Holy Ghost**. On the lesser level, you **receive** the Holy Ghost (we will talk more about that later on), and on the greater level, you are **filled** with the Holy Ghost, which is what the apostles experienced.

In this same manner, there are two levels of the **baptism in the Name of the Lord Jesus**. On the greater level, you receive the engrafted Word, which imparts the faith of the Son of God, who believes the Gospel of Perfection. On the lesser level, you receive the Holy Spirit and the faith to believe that the virile seed of Christ can be formed in you.

40

Those who have no relationship with Christ and no understanding of spiritual principles such as Satan, hell, and death, can hear the Gospel of the Cross and receive faith for salvation and **reconciliation** to God through the Lord Jesus Christ.

As we look at the Church world today, we see that many have received the lesser manifestation of the **baptism in the Name of the Lord Jesus** (faith to have Christ formed in them), and the lesser manifestation of the **baptism with the Holy Spirit** (virile seed not yet engrafted). But few have heard the **Doctrine of Christ**, which is going forth in this hour to bring the Church into spiritual maturity.

Spiritual Maturation

The Lord wants His Church baptized into the greater manifestation of the **baptism in the Name of the Lord Jesus** (the engrafted Word), and after that, He wants us to come under obedience so that He can *fill* us with the Holy Ghost (temporary full stature), whenever the purposes of the Kingdom of God require it.

Acts 13:9-11

⁹ THEN SAUL, (WHO ALSO IS CALLED PAUL,) **FILLED WITH THE HOLY GHOST**, SET HIS EYES ON HIM,

¹⁰ AND SAID, O FULL OF ALL SUBTILTY AND ALL MISCHIEF, THOU CHILD OF THE DEVIL, THOU ENEMY OF ALL RIGHTEOUSNESS, WILT THOU NOT CEASE TO PERVERT THE RIGHT WAYS OF THE LORD?

¹¹ AND NOW, BEHOLD, THE HAND OF THE LORD IS UPON THEE, AND THOU SHALT BE BLIND, NOT SEEING THE SUN FOR A SEASON. AND IMMEDIATELY THERE FELL ON HIM A MIST AND A DARKNESS; AND HE WENT ABOUT SEEKING SOME TO LEAD HIM BY THE HAND. **KJV**

QUESTION: Some people have a supernatural receiving of the Lord. Is that what you are talking about?

PASTOR VITALE: No, the ***baptism in the Name of the Lord Jesus*** is spiritual maturation. Our fallen nature is being reformed into the Lord Jesus Christ's image. People like you, for example, who have received the ***baptism with water*** and the Holy Ghost, are now receiving the ***baptism in the Name of the Lord Jesus***, which is a process that only God can do.

Our new spiritual nature is being formed like a fetus ***in utero,*** and our spiritual organs are appearing one at a time. At two weeks you have this organ, and at three weeks you have that organ, etc.

QUESTION: In other words, this teaching is going to create our new nature?

PASTOR VITALE: The true message of the Gospel of Perfection, which is not available everywhere at this time, is the fruit of the ***baptism in the Name of the Lord Jesus***. You would not be able to understand it if it were right in front of your nose, unless it is your time to experience it.

The large majority of believers are ruling their own lives and have no idea how important this baptism is. They think they can pick and choose where they go and what they do, so they are not likely to recognize that the Doctrine of Christ is from God.

Only those who will follow God anywhere, who are hungering and thirsting for Him, and seeking Him out with all their heart and soul, are moving into the Doctrine of Christ at this time.

Rev 14:4

[4] THESE ARE THEY WHICH WERE NOT DEFILED WITH WOMEN; FOR THEY ARE VIRGINS. THESE ARE **THEY WHICH FOLLOW THE LAMB WHITHERSOEVER HE GOETH**. THESE WERE REDEEMED FROM AMONG MEN, BEING THE FIRSTFRUITS UNTO GOD AND TO THE LAMB. **KJV**

The others are not willing to pay the price.

COMMENT: This makes me think of when Jesus came the first time. The Jews rejected Him because they expected Him to come in a particular way. Now, at the end time, everybody is expecting a great rapture and other things, and will not be in the place where they can receive what is really happening.

PASTOR VITALE: The Lord is bringing forth the Doctrine of Christ and offering it to those who will consider it, no matter what shape, manner, or form they are in when He calls them. They will receive the understanding because the others who think they can pick and choose how they serve God, follow after their own spirit.

Five Virgins

QUESTION: Isn't that like the five virgins?

PASTOR VITALE: Yes, there were five lamps filled, and five lamps not filled. Many are called, but are not filling up with the oil of Christ Jesus. They are the ones who will say, Why did you not tell me, Lord? And the Lord will say, I did not have to explain it to you. I called you. I said, Come. But you could not discern that it was Me talking through another person because you were not even looking for Me. You did not believe I would talk to you through anyone other than yourself. You were too busy running your own life. There will be wailing and gnashing of teeth.

Gospel of Perfection

Getting back to our subject, I think there are very few believers who are maturing into Christ in this hour, but many are maturing in their carnal mind. The reason we see the greater manifestation of baptism in the Book of Acts, is that Paul was there to preach the true *Gospel of God*.

The Lord told me to call this message the *Gospel of Perfection*, because there are so many preachers out there preaching a counterfeit *Gospel of the Kingdom*.

Paul preached the *Gospel of Perfection* to the believers in the Book of Acts, but until this present time, the true *Gospel of Perfection* has not been available to the Church world. On the contrary, many are preaching that you cannot become perfect, but true spiritual maturity is perfection.

COMMENT: When we think of perfection, we think of being so perfect that we are like God, but maturity allows for some mistakes.

PASTOR VITALE: This is not true, and it is where a lot of people lose their understanding. *God is not perfecting our sin nature. He is killing our sin nature, and replacing it with His nature.* Christ, the Son of God in us, is our perfection.

Think of yourself as an empty shell filled with duck feathers. The Lord Jesus is getting rid of all the duck feathers and filling us up with foam rubber. We will look the same, have the same family, the same job, and live in the same house, but our spiritual insides, which is our mind, will have been totally renovated. This is the spiritual maturity known as *perfection*.

Our righteousness is in Christ, but our carnal mind (sin nature) will not give us up. Our personality is female in relationship to our mind. Paul says,

> *Rom. 7:3 – AT:* If **[a woman] is married to another man** while her husband [the carnal mind] is still alive, she shall be called an adulteress. But if her husband is dead [because of the righteousness of Christ Jesus], the law does not apply to her, and she is not an adulteress, even though she is married to another man (**ATB**).

To answer your question, I think there are very few people in this hour who have received the *Gospel of Perfection* simply because, to the best of my knowledge, its availability is very limited.

You will not understand the doctrine if you have other gods before you. Neither will you understand it if your motive is wrong, even if you are present every time Christ preaches. The Lord Jesus is in control. You cannot steal the things of God.

Do you have any idea how many people think they can steal the things of God? Some actually believe that they can steal another believer's gifts. Simon the sorcerer thought that he could buy the Holy Ghost.

Acts 8:18-19

> [18] AND WHEN SIMON SAW THAT THROUGH LAYING ON OF THE APOSTLES' HANDS THE HOLY GHOST WAS GIVEN, **HE OFFERED THEM MONEY,**
>
> [19] SAYING, GIVE ME ALSO THIS POWER, THAT ON WHOMSOEVER I LAY HANDS, HE MAY RECEIVE THE HOLY GHOST. **KJV**

It is the ignorance of the carnal mind. That is what we are up against, the ignorance of the carnal mind.

Paul preached the ***Gospel of Perfection*** to the disciples at Ephesus, and they were baptized in the Name, or the Spirit, of the Lord Jesus Christ when they heard the Word. Their human spirit received the fertilized virile seed of the Father, and the second generation of Christ began to be formed in them. That is how the Kingdom of God is imparted to us. The Kingdom of God is Christ in you, the hope of glory,

Col 1:27

> [27] TO WHOM GOD WOULD MAKE KNOWN WHAT IS THE RICHES OF THE GLORY OF THIS MYSTERY AMONG THE GENTILES; WHICH IS CHRIST IN YOU, THE HOPE OF GLORY: **KJV**

Verse 6, ***Paul laid hands on them and the Holy Ghost came upon them***. The Scripture does not say that they were baptized. It says that ***the Holy Ghost came upon them***.

Acts 19:6

> [6] AND WHEN PAUL HAD LAID HIS HANDS UPON THEM, THE HOLY GHOST CAME ON THEM; AND THEY SPAKE WITH TONGUES, AND PROPHESIED. **KJV**

The Greek word translated ***came***, means to ***arise,*** or to ***appear***.

The indication here is that Christ was already within the Jews who heard the ***Gospel of the Kingdom***. When they believed, the Holy Ghost came upon them, and Christ arose. The believing Jews experienced the resurrection of Christ by speaking in tongues and prophesying.

It is a great mystery that Christ is both an inherited seed and a new seed of the Lord Jesus. The seed that Jews inherit from Abraham . . .

Gal 3:16

> [16] NOW TO ABRAHAM AND HIS SEED WERE THE PROMISES MADE. HE SAITH NOT, AND TO SEEDS, AS OF MANY; BUT AS OF ONE, AND TO THY SEED, WHICH IS CHRIST. **KJV**

. . . is a female seed, and the seed that we inherit from the Lord Jesus is both male and female. It is a fertilized seed, fully equipped to regenerate Righteous Adam [Christ Jesus] in the individual.

Spiritual Perfection

COMMENT: At the beginning of my walk the Lord said, When I call, will you come? I thought He was calling me to the rapture!

PASTOR VITALE: It does not matter how messed up we are by false doctrine or misunderstanding. The heart that is hungering and thirsting for Christ will find Him, because we want Him so much that we pursue the slightest hint that this *new thing* might be Him. We will not be left behind.

COMMENT: I thought of coming out of one church, and then out of another church, was part of the maturation process. I thought each church was a different calling, but to finally be nowhere but in my own home, it gets more and more lonely.

PASTOR VITALE: Yes, tell me about it! It is a very lonely walk, and the testing is severe, but it is certainly worth it in view of what He is offering us. I do not know many Christians that really have a vision of what God is offering us. But even those who understand, do not really believe that *spiritual perfection* is possible in their lifetime. Spiritual maturity in Christ Jesus is available in our lifetime. It is real.

In my opinion, the large majority of people that believe in *Sonship* and *Ultimate Reconciliation* are not moving into *spiritual perfection* because they are embracing a false message.

Spiritual perfection requires hearing and believing the *Gospel of Perfection*, as it is preached under the anointing. If you believe in *Sonship*, but also believe that those outside of Christ will burn in hell forever, you do not believe the true *Gospel of God.*

If you believe in *Ultimate Reconciliation*, but also believe that you do not have a sin nature, or do not have to wage war against your carnal mind, or that you will ascend automatically, you do not believe *the true Gospel of God.*

Both camps are embracing a false gospel. I do not care how much it sounds like the real thing, mixture is anti-Christ. You either have the true message, or you do not. You either have the Lord Jesus Christ's virile seed, or you have a corrupt seed which can produce only death. This is hard work.

COMMENT: I can see why the enemy does not want people to hear this message. It will set them free.

PASTOR VITALE: Yes. It used to bother me when someone rejected this message, but it does not bother me anymore. I am still maturing in Christ myself. You get to the place, eventually, where you do what the Lord tells you to do, one day at a time.

Following the Call of God

This morning Barbara made breakfast for Rosemary and I, and asked me if I would drive her to the library. I did not know I would be preaching tonight, but I did know that the Lord had taken hold of me, because I had already started to study. I did not know how to tell Barbara *no*, because I was a guest in her mother-in-law's house, so I said *okay* without even praying about it. But as I went back to my studies, the Lord seized me with even greater strength.

Barbara came down the steps an hour later and told me to forget it, because she could not make it to the library herself. I did not even pray about it. But God knew that my heart was turned towards Him, and took care of it. He will do the same thing with your husbands, and with your children. He will make a way if you are truly willing to turn your life over to Him.

Either He is the Lord of your life, or He is not the Lord of your life. I declare to you that Jesus is not Lord over the life of anyone who decides they cannot come to a meeting called by special appointment, without first asking if He wants them to go.

Now, you need to have spiritual discernment. I am not talking about preachers who try to force you to come to their meetings. A preacher calling you because he wants his church filled up, is one thing. But when Jesus calls a meeting, you should be willing to obey the Lord if He makes a way. You just say, Lord, if you want me to go, make a way. Then, if a door does not open, your conscience is clear. But you have to pray the prayer.

COMMENT: It is funny that you should talk about this. I made all those phone calls inviting people to the meeting, and then sat down to read. But I was convicted, so I made more phone calls. It made me think of the Scripture, *Compel them to come in*, but they do not want to.

PASTOR VITALE: Most will not come, because they have no understanding.

There was an evangelist from Florida in my area about eight months ago. I usually do not go to those meetings, but when someone called me up to tell me about the meetings, I did the same thing that all those who did not come today did. I said, *I do not think I will go*, without praying about it. God knows that my heart is truly turned towards Him, but that I make mistakes from time to time, so He had mercy on me.

Late in the evening (too late to be going out for no reason), I started driving around in my car without knowing where I was going. I wound up in front of the church where this evangelist would be preaching. It was closed, but I got out of the car and went towards the church thinking, *Lord, what am I doing here*? As I approached the glass doors, I saw that there was a flyer posted on the door advertising an evangelist. As soon as I looked at it, I knew that this was the same evangelist that I had decided not to go see, and realized that the Lord was telling me to go.

This Church has two meetings on Sunday: 8:30 a.m. and 10:30 a.m. I went to the 8:30 a.m. meeting, but was convicted to go back for the 10:30 a.m. meeting. After that, I attended every day.

He preached seven meetings, and the last one was for financial miracles -- at a time that I needed a financial miracle. I decided to go, and to call several people that the Lord told me to invite.

I knew that one couple was having severe financial difficulties, and said to them, **The Lord told me to tell you to come**. I guess they did not believe me when I said, **God told me**, because they were too busy to come.

Then I called another woman who, to the best of my knowledge, had no financial problems. She said, **Oh, you mean the Lord told you to call me?** I said, **Yes**, but she did not come either, and the next time I saw her she apologized to me.

I said, **You do not have to apologize to me, I called for you, not for me.** She then went on to tell me, without even realizing what she was saying, what a dire financial need she had. This woman, who is a mature believer, had no understanding that God intended to meet her need in that service.

She knows that I am a woman of God, but she could not connect to what I said. She could not believe that God might have really told me to tell her to come, and that He intended to answer her need through that man's ministry.

What is the problem? The problem is the lie circulating in the Church today, that if you have any maturity in Christ, you do not have to go to church.

Of course, you do not have to go to church if God tells you not to go. But if you have been praying about a dire financial need for six months, and God says, **I will meet your need through this evangelist from Florida**, you should be running to that church. Whatever God was intending to do for you through that ministry is lost, if you do not go when He calls you.

Will God not help you another way? Maybe He will, but maybe He will not. It depends upon the attitude of your heart. Will you recognize the Lord's next attempt to answer your prayer? How long will it take you to lay hold of His supernatural provision, if you cannot recognize it when it manifests?

There is another false doctrine circulating among mature believers today, many of whom have been called out. They think that in this hour, Christ is manifesting Himself to them only through themselves. This is a very dangerous belief. The truth is that the Lord Jesus can meet your needs however He wants to -- and that includes through other believers.

We must be ready to get up and move when He calls us, because Christ is manifesting in the many members of the body of Christ. Some people have gifts that others do not have. Some have the gift of healing, others have the gift of financial blessings. This is true. To think that you do not need the ministry that God has placed in another believer, is a high manifestation of pride.

The Holy Spirit - A Taste of Baptism

The Gospel of the Cross, the message preached in the Church today, imparts the faith to believe that there is *salvation in the Name of the Lord Jesus Christ*.

Water baptism, the lesser baptism in the Name of the Lord Jesus, imparts *the Holy Ghost* and *faith to believe that Christ can be resurrected in the individual*.

What am I saying? The Church is not experiencing the *BAPTISM with the Holy Ghost* today. The Church is *RECEIVING*, or *EXPERIENCING*, the Holy Ghost.

The Church is also experiencing a measure of the *baptism in the Name of the Lord Jesus*, which *engrafts the virile seed of the Lord Jesus Christ* to the human spirit. It also promises the Holy Ghost to those who believe the *Gospel of Perfection*. This is Jesus speaking to the apostles,

Acts 1:5

> [5] FOR JOHN TRULY BAPTIZED WITH WATER; BUT YE SHALL BE **BAPTIZED WITH THE HOLY GHOST** NOT MANY DAYS HENCE. **KJV**

Jesus did not say they would ***RECEIVE*** the Holy Ghost, nor did He say that the Holy Ghost would ***COME UPON THEM***. Jesus said to the apostles, Ye shall be ***BAPTIZED*** with the Holy Ghost.

Cornelius

Peter preached the ***Gospel of the Cross*** to Cornelius and the Italian band, and they experienced the Holy Ghost.

Acts 10:38-39

> [38] HOW **GOD ANOINTED JESUS OF NAZARETH WITH THE HOLY GHOST AND WITH POWER**: WHO WENT ABOUT DOING GOOD, AND HEALING ALL THAT WERE OPPRESSED OF THE DEVIL; FOR GOD WAS WITH HIM.
>
> [39] AND WE ARE WITNESSES OF ALL THINGS WHICH HE DID BOTH IN THE LAND OF THE JEWS, AND IN JERUSALEM; WHOM THEY SLEW AND HANGED ON A TREE: **KJV**

Peter is not preaching the Gospel of Perfection to the Gentiles. ***The Gospel of Perfection is preached to the Jew***. John the Baptist water baptized the Jews, but ***the Gentiles heard the Gospel of the Cross***.

Acts 10:44

> [44] WHILE PETER YET SPAKE THESE WORDS, **THE HOLY GHOST FELL ON ALL THEM**. . . . **KJV**

The Gospel of the Cross Is For The Gentiles

The Gentiles were not **BAPTIZED** with the Holy Ghost. The Holy Ghost **FELL ON THE GENTILES** who had no knowledge of the Scripture. That Greek word means to be **seized forcibly**, or **laid hold of.** The Holy Ghost forcibly seized the men who heard the Gospel of the Cross preached, and seized their carnal mind.

The Gospel Of The Kingdom Is For The Jew

The **Gospel of the Kingdom, the message that Christ can be formed in the individual,** is preached to the Jew or the Gentile who believes that the Lord Jesus is the Son of God. When it is understood that Christ can be formed in them also, the Holy Spirit is given to raise Christ, Abraham's seed in them, from the dead.

I suggest to you that the Holy Spirit, as we see it in the Church today, is the same measure of the Holy Spirit that supernaturally discerned that Christ could be raised in Cornelius and his band when they heard the **Gospel of the Cross**.

The message of a **personal savior**, not the message that Christ can be formed in you, **imparts the Holy Spirit without seed**. The message of a personal savior imparts **a basic understanding of God's plan for mankind through Jesus Christ**.

The message that Christ can be formed in the individual imparts a mature understanding of how it can happen.

The Gospel of the cross and the Gospel of the Kingdom are two aspects of a single message.

53

Acts 10:45

⁴⁵ AND THEY OF THE CIRCUMCISION WHICH BELIEVED WERE ASTONISHED, AS MANY AS CAME WITH PETER, BECAUSE THAT ON THE GENTILES ALSO WAS **POURED OUT THE GIFT OF THE HOLY GHOST. KJV**

Not *BAPTIZED WITH*, but *POURED OUT UPON*. The gift of the Holy Ghost was poured out upon them from Peter, and they knew what had happened,

Acts 10:46

⁴⁶ FOR **THEY HEARD THEM SPEAK WITH TONGUES,** AND MAGNIFY GOD. . . . **KJV**

QUESTION: Is water baptism the seal?

PASTOR VITALE: Water baptism is a sign or token that Jesus made a covenant with you. You do your little kindergarten scribble, and Jesus does the rest. That is the size of it.

The true Jew has the *Gospel of the Kingdom*. If you are receiving the *Gospel of the Kingdom* in this hour, you are a true Jew. Many in the Church today have not heard, or do not believe, the *Gospel of Perfection*. These uncircumcised (spiritual) Jews are still controlled by their carnal mind, even though they may have received the Holy Spirit.

First Fruits Company

Do not be concerned if you have not heard or do not understand the *Gospel of Perfection*. Just ask the Lord Jesus for it.

Do not be deceived, though. A knowledge of the *Gospel of Perfection* will surely bring the fiery trials that expose your sin nature upon you.

1 Peter 4:12

> [12] BELOVED, THINK IT NOT STRANGE CONCERNING **THE FIERY TRIAL WHICH IS TO TRY YOU,** AS THOUGH SOME STRANGE THING HAPPENED UNTO YOU: **KJV**

Such trials are your opportunity to repent of specific sin and overcome your carnal mind, a major requirement for going on to perfection.

Jehovah is a good and a merciful God. He will restore this entire creation, through the Lord Jesus Christ, to a greater spiritual maturity than Adam had when he failed to distinguish between his good and evil selves. Everyone will not ascend at the same time. Each man will be restored to spiritual maturity as the Lord calls him. But there will be a *First Fruits Company of believers who* arise to help those who come after them.

This message, that some will ascend before others, offends some Christians who perceive it to be an elitist message. But does not this same relationship exist today between those who have already received the Lord Jesus as Savior, and those who have not? And is there not a First Fruits Company which has received the Holy Ghost before the others who are to follow?

Spiritual Intimacy

QUESTION: Is Jesus' statement, *I never knew you*, similar?

PASTOR VITALE: When Jesus said, *I never knew you*, He was talking about spiritual intimacy. Experiencing the Holy Ghost is not the same thing as marriage to the Lord Jesus.

The Holy Spirit forms personal relationships with the carnal mind of mortal men, but the Lord Jesus who is above, engages in spiritual intimacy with the Christ Mind. Christ must be raised in the individual, either by faith, or by graft, before we can have intimacy with the Lord Jesus.

The Holy Spirit, which carries the seed of the Lord Jesus, is given to establish a relationship with the human spirit and raise Christ in the men who receive him. The oil of Christ Jesus, Who is above, then smears together with the maturing Christ in the individual. *Christ raised in the individual, not the Holy Spirit, is our personal Savior*, and our new life, which is rooted and grounded in righteousness.

Christ Jesus Is Savior

If you believe that the Holy Spirit can meet all of your spiritual needs, you are like one who says, *I do not want to be involved in my own deliverance, just knock all these demons out of me, and I will be okay.*

The Lord Jesus wants a bride from His own family line, which is Christ in us. Our carnal mind, which is an alien, a stranger to Him, will not satisfy Him.

Gen 24:3-4

> [3] AND I WILL MAKE THEE SWEAR BY THE LORD, THE GOD OF HEAVEN, AND THE GOD OF THE EARTH, THAT **THOU SHALT NOT TAKE A WIFE UNTO MY SON OF THE DAUGHTERS OF THE CANAANITES**, AMONG WHOM I DWELL:

> [4] BUT THOU SHALT GO UNTO MY COUNTRY, AND TO MY KINDRED, AND **TAKE A WIFE UNTO MY SON ISAAC**. **KJV**

I recently read in a well-known ministry newsletter, that two spiritual powers are fighting over humanity, but we do not have an active part in the war. Any message that teaches passivity to the body of Christ is a lie.

When Christ bombs Satan we feel it, and when Satan bombs Christ we feel it. We are right in the middle of this war, and our decision to line up with Satan, or with Christ, affects the outcome of our whole life.

The Personality Is Not Resurrected

QUESTION: Why would we need the armor if we were not part of the war?

PASTOR VITALE: We are a part of the war. We participate in the war by choosing which side we align ourselves with.

The time for Christ to appear in the multitude is very near, but as the true doctrine comes forth, heresies are also appearing.

1 Cor 11:19

> [19] FOR **THERE MUST BE ALSO HERESIES AMONG YOU,** THAT THEY WHICH ARE APPROVED MAY BE MADE MANIFEST AMONG YOU. **KJV**

Ministries that have taught sound doctrine for 20 and 30 years are falling into false doctrine. The truth is very hard. Some people get upset with the teaching that the personality is not resurrected, especially if they are holding on to the memory of a dead loved one, a mother, or a husband, for example.

We are supposed to be dying to self and living unto Christ, so that the purposes of God are accomplished through us. If the thought of seeing your mother, or any other dead loved one when you get to the other side, is keeping you alive, that desire is an idol in your heart. A lot of people have a problem with that.

Christ Is The Only Reality

Paul called the things of this world ***dung***, saying that the maturation of Christ is the only significant thing.

Phil 3:8

> [8] YEA DOUBTLESS, AND I COUNT ALL THINGS BUT LOSS FOR THE EXCELLENCY OF THE KNOWLEDGE OF CHRIST JESUS MY LORD: FOR WHOM **I HAVE SUFFERED THE LOSS OF ALL THINGS, AND DO COUNT THEM BUT DUNG**, THAT I MAY WIN CHRIST, **KJV**

Paul knew that every other aspect of this temporal life will cease to exist, either when the individual dies, or when this age rolls up like a scroll and goes out like a light. Only Christ will continue to mature until Christ Jesus appears in that last generation.

Christ is the only reality. Our life is valuable because Christ lives in us. We no longer identity with our physical body or our emotions after we give our personality over to Christ.

Christ is in us, but because He is so immature, we frequently cannot understand, or believe this truth. We can measure the penetration of Christ into our everyday lives by the extent that the idols in our heart have been crushed.

Ezek 14:3

> [3] SON OF MAN, **THESE MEN HAVE SET UP THEIR IDOLS IN THEIR HEART,** AND PUT THE STUMBLINGBLOCK OF

THEIR INIQUITY BEFORE THEIR FACE: SHOULD I BE INQUIRED
OF AT ALL BY THEM? **KJV**

Physical Water, Spiritual Water

Acts 10:44-45

[44] WHILE PETER YET SPAKE THESE WORDS, THE
HOLY GHOST FELL[1] ON ALL THEM.

[45] AND THEY OF THE CIRCUMCISION WHICH
BELIEVED WERE ASTONISHED, AS MANY AS CAME WITH
PETER, BECAUSE THAT **ON THE GENTILES ALSO WAS
POURED OUT**[2] **THE GIFT OF THE HOLY GHOST. KJV**

The physical body is submerged under *physical* water in water
baptism, but in the *baptism with the Holy Ghost*, spiritual water
is poured out over the carnal mind, which is a spiritual body.

In the *first stage* of the *baptism With the Holy Ghost*, we *receive*
the Holy Ghost.

Acts 10:47

[47] CAN ANY MAN FORBID WATER, THAT THESE
SHOULD NOT BE BAPTIZED, **WHICH HAVE RECEIVED**[3] **THE
HOLY GHOST** AS WELL AS WE? **KJV**

---

[1] The Greek word translated *fell on*, Strong's #1968, means, *to be seized
violently.*

[2] The Greek word translated *poured,* Strong's #1632, means, *to spill or
gush over like water*.

[3] The word, *receive*, Strong's #2983, means, *to get a knowledge of.*

This means that people like us who speak in tongues and prophesy occasionally, ***have a knowledge of the Holy Ghost***, but the apostles were ***baptized*** and ***filled with*** the Holy Ghost.

Filled With The Holy Ghost

The word ***filled*** means to ***fill up completely, to satisfy***, or ***to complete***.

The Holy Ghost ***completed*** the apostles. This means that the male seed of the Lord Jesus was added to the female Christ seed that the apostles had inherited from Abraham. It does not mean that the seed that they received ***grafted*** to their human spirit.

The term ***anointed*** with the Holy Ghost signifies the **ENGRAFTED** spiritual maturity that Jesus of Nazareth experienced. Today's Christians have ***received*** a measure of the Holy Ghost. They are not filled with it.

COMMENT: I thought ***to be filled*** means ***to be led***.

PASTOR VITALE: Yes, that definition is taught in the Church today. The Church also teaches that we need to be ***refilled*** with the Holy Ghost when our spiritual walk slows down. But I cannot find either of those teachings in the Bible.

The apostles were ***filled*** with the Holy Ghost, and Jesus' seed grafted to their human spirit and completed ***Christ*** who was already formed in them, ***by faith***.

The spiritual strength and power that the apostles received when the Holy Ghost came upon them . . .

Acts 1:8

> [8] BUT YE SHALL RECEIVE POWER, AFTER THAT
> THE HOLY GHOST IS COME UPON YOU: AND YE SHALL BE

. . . were in the fully resurrected Christ. The manchild is the only legitimate witness . . .

1 Tim 2:15

15 NOTWITHSTANDING **SHE SHALL BE SAVED IN CHILDBEARING,** IF THEY CONTINUE IN FAITH AND CHARITY AND HOLINESS WITH SOBRIETY. **KJV**

Rev 12:4

4 AND HIS TAIL DREW THE THIRD PART OF THE STARS OF HEAVEN, AND DID CAST THEM TO THE EARTH: AND **THE DRAGON STOOD BEFORE THE WOMAN WHICH WAS READY TO BE DELIVERED,** FOR TO DEVOUR HER CHILD AS SOON AS IT WAS BORN. **KJV**

. . . to Jesus' resurrection.

Acts 4:30

30 BY STRETCHING FORTH THINE HAND TO HEAL; AND THAT SIGNS AND WONDERS MAY BE DONE **BY THE NAME OF THY HOLY CHILD JESUS. KJV**

Christ cannot be completed in the Christians *receiving* the Holy Ghost because He is not yet formed in them. The Holy Spirit imparts *the power to be made strong*, that is, to have Christ formed in them.

Who are you, Sheila, to say that today's Christians do not have Christ formed in them? The proof of the pudding is in the power. There is no manifestation of power that I know of in today's Church that equals the power demonstrated by the apostles.

61

Acts 2:4

> [4] AND [the apostles] WERE ALL FILLED[4] WITH THE HOLY GHOST, AND BEGAN TO SPEAK WITH OTHER TONGUES, AS THE SPIRIT GAVE THEM UTTERANCE. **KJV**

The apostles were no longer *experiencing* the Holy Ghost, but were being *influenced* by it to do something.

The gifts of the Spirit *acquaint us* with the Holy Ghost, and we *experience* the Holy Ghost as we exercise the gifts. But, the Holy Ghost *influences* us only to the extent that we obey it.

1 Cor 12:4-7

> [4] NOW THERE ARE **DIVERSITIES OF GIFTS**, BUT THE SAME SPIRIT.
>
> [5] AND THERE ARE **DIFFERENCES OF ADMINISTRATIONS**, BUT THE SAME LORD.
>
> [6] AND THERE ARE **DIVERSITIES OF OPERATIONS,** BUT IT IS THE SAME GOD WHICH WORKETH ALL IN ALL.
>
> [7] BUT **THE MANIFESTATION OF THE SPIRIT IS GIVEN TO EVERY MAN TO PROFIT WITHAL. KJV**

Again, those who *received* the Holy Ghost and *experienced* it spoke in tongues and prophesied, *but the apostles were influenced to do something*.

The word *filled*, also means to *satiate*, *to fill up*, and suggests *taking full possession of the mind*. The Holy Spirit took full possession of the apostles' mind, but this is not what happened to Cornelius and the Italian band. They only *experienced* it.

---

[4]   The word, *filled*, Strong's #4130, means *to be influenced by.*

Speaking in tongues, prophesying, and the word of knowledge are *experiences* in the Holy Ghost. Pride carries away many who have these gifts, but the truth is that Holy Ghost *experiences* are free gifts that require no skill or accomplishment of any kind. The gifts are not a reward.

Baptism with the Holy Ghost means that the Holy Spirit takes full possession of your mind. The sign that the Holy Ghost took full possession of the apostles' mind, is that they spoke in *other* tongues.

Seized By The Holy Ghost

We can tell Jesus that we would like to become *acquainted* with His Holy Spirit, but Jesus is the one who decides whether or not His Spirit will seize us, so that we can receive it.

COMMENT: What does that mean, *fell on violently*?

PASTOR VITALE:

Acts 10:44

> [44] WHILE PETER YET SPAKE THESE WORDS, **THE HOLY GHOST FELL[5] ON ALL THEM WHICH HEARD THE WORD. KJV**

Peter spoke the Word, the Holy Spirit stretched out and fell upon them violently and possessed them, and that is how they became *acquainted* with the Holy Ghost. This sure is a far cry from fallen man deciding whether or not he receives the Holy Ghost!

---

[5]   The Greek word translated *fell*, Strong's #1968, means to be *seized violently.*

Acts 10:48

> [48] AND HE COMMANDED[6] THEM TO BE BAPTIZED
> IN THE NAME OF THE LORD. . . . KJV

The Scripture says, Peter *commanded*, but we do not know whether Peter spoke in words, or thought a spiritual command. Verbalized speech is for spiritually immature people, and that includes me.

I use language because my Christ Mind is too immature to communicate my thoughts directly to your mind. The Lord speaks to us with an audible voice occasionally, but prefers directing us to a particular Scripture, or showing us symbols *in the Spirit*, with mind-to-mind communication. This world is in a very low spiritual dimension.

The foundation of our salvation, which is the Lord Jesus Christ, is set in the hearts of men. Christ Jesus, the spiritual authority within Peter, imparted a spiritual seed which grafted to the human spirit of these men. That seed then became the foundation upon which their salvation, Christ within them, would be built.

The Holy Ghost fell upon Cornelius and his band, and Peter, an apostle that Christ was complete in, commanded that Jesus' virile seed should engraft to their human spirit.

In this hour, the Church is experiencing *reconciliation*. That is, faith in the Lord Jesus, as Savior, by the preaching of the Gospel of the Cross, water baptism, and the receiving of (becoming acquainted with) the Holy Ghost.

---

[6] The Greek word translated, *commanded*, Strong's #4367, comes from two other Greek words which mean *to come near to*, or *to set in order, to assign*.

The Holy Ghost is the lesser manifestation of the **baptism in the Name of the Lord Jesus**, which is the faith to have Christ formed in you. The greater manifestation of the **baptism in the Name of the Lord Jesus**, is the engrafted Word.

As far as I know, the full **baptism with the Holy Ghost** is very rare today, if anyone is experiencing it at all, and no one is **anointed of the Holy Ghost**, which is engrafted spiritual completion.

The Seed Of The Manchild

Humanity will be saved when the manchild is born in each individual member of the human race. **Spiritual fertilization** is the conception of the embryonic Christ by the engrafting of Jesus' virile seed to the individual human spirit. Jesus likened **spiritual fertilization** to the **lighting of a candle**.

<u>Matt 5:15</u>

> [15] NEITHER DO MEN LIGHT A CANDLE, AND PUT IT UNDER A BUSHEL, BUT ON A CANDLESTICK; AND **IT GIVETH LIGHT UNTO ALL THAT ARE IN THE HOUSE. KJV**

Our Father is reproducing His nature in mankind. When I say, *fertilized*, I mean that Jesus' spiritual seed, which is carried by the Holy Ghost, penetrated the human spirit and joined itself to Christ, Abraham's seed. This two-fold union forms the foundation of the new nature in our mind.

Perhaps what happened between Peter and these men was similar to what I experienced last night. I felt like my mind was a machine gun shooting at someone, saying, **Be fertilized, be fertilized.** The Lord initiated the experience, so I guess he was fertilized, but you never know how long it will take for the seed to sprout.

TONGUES

I [Paul] speak in the TONGUES OF MEN and I speak in the TONGUES OF ANGELS.

1 Cor 13:1

> [1] THOUGH I SPEAK WITH THE **TONGUES OF MEN** AND OF ANGELS. . . . **KJV**

Tongues of Men (Other Tongues)

Other Tongues are known human languages. To speak with *tongues of men* (other tongues) is the supernatural ability to speak in known, human languages of which you have no personal knowledge.

The apostles were *baptized*, or completely *filled,* with the Holy Ghost, which means that *their carnal mind came under Jesus' complete control*, and they spoke in languages which were foreign to them.

Tongues of Men (other tongues) are the Scriptural witness to the *baptism with the Holy Ghost*, which so fully matures the Christ Mind, that the carnal mind is repressed.

Reports of Christians speaking in *foreign languages* for one conversation, or whatever length of time it takes to fulfill the Lord's specific purpose, circulate through the Church periodically. I heard one testimony where an evangelist who was empowered to speak Spanish for one service retained that ability.

Tongues of Angels (New Tongues)

New tongues are the personal prayer language by which the newly conceived Christ Mind communicates with the Jesus.

<u>Mark 16:17</u>

> [17] AND THESE SIGNS SHALL FOLLOW THEM THAT BELIEVE; IN MY NAME SHALL THEY CAST OUT DEVILS; **THEY SHALL SPEAK WITH NEW TONGUES;**[7] **KJV**

Cornelius and the Italian band *received* the Holy Ghost and spoke in *tongues of angels,* or *new tongues*.

Angel tongues, or *new tongues*, must be superior to human tongues, because everything that God does is superior to the works of the carnal mind.

New tongues are the Scriptural witness that we have *received* the Holy Ghost.

We become *acquainted* with the Holy Ghost in its lesser manifestation by supernaturally experiencing the gifts of the Spirit. But we cannot stop there, because *experiencing* the Holy Ghost is spiritual baby stuff. There is more. That is why, as we mature in Christ, the gifts begin to disappear. It is grow-up time.

---

[7] The word *new*, Strong's #2537, means *recently made tongues*, suggesting that what is newly, or recently made, is superior to that which is replaced.

1 Cor 13:8-12

⁸ CHARITY NEVER FAILETH: BUT WHETHER THERE BE **PROPHECIES, THEY SHALL FAIL**; WHETHER THERE BE **TONGUES, THEY SHALL CEASE**; WHETHER THERE BE **KNOWLEDGE, IT SHALL VANISH AWAY.**

⁹ FOR WE KNOW IN PART, AND WE PROPHESY IN PART.

¹⁰ BUT **WHEN THAT WHICH IS PERFECT IS COME, THEN THAT WHICH IS IN PART SHALL BE DONE AWAY.**

¹¹ WHEN I WAS A CHILD, I SPAKE AS A CHILD, I UNDERSTOOD AS A CHILD, I THOUGHT AS A CHILD: BUT **WHEN I BECAME A MAN, I PUT AWAY CHILDISH THINGS.**

¹² FOR NOW WE SEE THROUGH A GLASS, DARKLY; BUT THEN FACE TO FACE: **NOW I KNOW IN PART; BUT THEN SHALL I KNOW EVEN AS ALSO I AM KNOWN. KJV**

Prophetic Utterances in Tongues

There are personal and public *new tongues*.

New tongues are spiritual languages which must be interpreted, because there is no translation.

Translation is a word-by-word conversion from one language to another. *Interpretation* is the *essence* of the message, as the interpreter perceives it.

It would be highly unlikely for a Chinese person, for example, to understand a public utterance of tongues. This could happen, but if it did, the utterance would be *other tongues* and not *new tongues*.

Some Scriptures say *new tongues*, some say *other tongues*, but the majority just say *tongues*, so we have to ask the Holy Ghost which tongues are manifesting in each specific case.

Acts 10:38

> [38] HOW **GOD ANOINTED JESUS OF NAZARETH WITH THE HOLY GHOST AND WITH POWER**: WHO WENT ABOUT DOING GOOD, AND HEALING ALL THAT WERE OPPRESSED OF THE DEVIL; FOR GOD WAS WITH HIM. **KJV**

There is a third stage of baptism that fills us with the Holy Ghost *permanently*. To be *anointed* with the Holy Ghost**,** means *to be smeared*, or *covered over permanently,* to the point that *it sticks to you*. This anointing does not rise up and subside, it rises up and sticks to you.

Different Kinds of Tongues

Here are some Scriptures to clarify the different kind of tongues.

Paul said that he spoke in both the *tongues of men* and the *tongues of angels*.

1 Cor 13:1

> [13] THOUGH **I SPEAK WITH THE TONGUES OF MEN AND OF ANGELS**, AND HAVE NOT CHARITY, I AM BECOME AS SOUNDING BRASS, OR A TINKLING CYMBAL. **KJV**

Tongues of men are identified as *other tongues* or *human languages* in,

Acts 2:4

⁴ AND THEY WERE ALL FILLED WITH THE HOLY GHOST, AND **BEGAN TO SPEAK WITH OTHER TONGUES,** AS THE SPIRIT GAVE THEM UTTERANCE. **KJV**

We see the phrase, ***diversities of tongues***, referring to various ***human languages*** in,

1 Cor 12:10

¹⁰ TO ANOTHER THE WORKING OF MIRACLES; TO ANOTHER PROPHECY; TO ANOTHER DISCERNING OF SPIRITS; TO **ANOTHER DIVERS KINDS OF TONGUES**; TO ANOTHER THE INTERPRETATION OF TONGUES: **KJV**

1 Cor 12:28

²⁸ AND GOD HATH SET SOME IN THE CHURCH, FIRST APOSTLES, SECONDARILY PROPHETS, THIRDLY TEACHERS, AFTER THAT MIRACLES, THEN GIFTS OF HEALINGS, HELPS, GOVERNMENTS, **DIVERSITIES OF TONGUES**. **KJV**

Tongues of angels are described as ***new tongues*** in,

Mark 16:17

¹⁷ AND THESE SIGNS SHALL FOLLOW THEM THAT BELIEVE; IN MY NAME SHALL THEY CAST OUT DEVILS; **THEY SHALL SPEAK WITH NEW TONGUES**; **KJV**

Tongues are always ***spoken***,

Acts 10:46

⁴⁶ **FOR THEY HEARD THEM SPEAK WITH TONGUES,** AND MAGNIFY GOD. THEN ANSWERED PETER, **KJV**

71

Acts 19:6

> ⁶ AND WHEN PAUL HAD LAID HIS HANDS UPON
> THEM, THE HOLY GHOST CAME ON THEM; AND **THEY SPAKE
> WITH TONGUES, AND PROPHESIED. KJV**

But sometimes they are ***HEARD***,

Acts 10:46

> ⁴⁶ FOR **THEY HEARD THEM SPEAK WITH TONGUES,**
> AND MAGNIFY GOD. THEN ANSWERED PETER, **KJV**

The word ***speak,*** in the Greek, refers to a ***discourse***. The reference books say that this word means ***designed to arouse emotion***, as opposed to casual conversation.

An utterance with tongues brought forth in the Church is a public discourse which usually has emotion and excitement associated with it. It is rarely, if ever, delivered in a conversational tone.

Tongues of angels refer to utterances with tongues that we can expect to be interpreted.

I will show you later on that the personal prayer language that we receive is not a gift. We are talking about gifts now.

I recently had an encounter with a man who keeps telling me that tongues is the least of all gifts, so who would want it? I told him, ***I want everything***. I want the greatest gift, and I want the least gift, but your personal prayer language is not a gift. Your personal prayer language is what you receive when the Holy Ghost is within you. It is for your personal communication with the Lord.

The men from Cornelius' band spoke in tongues which were loud and public.

1 Cor 12:10

> [10] TO ANOTHER THE WORKING OF MIRACLES; TO ANOTHER PROPHECY; TO ANOTHER DISCERNING OF SPIRITS; TO **ANOTHER DIVERS KINDS OF TONGUES**; TO ANOTHER THE **INTERPRETATION OF TONGUES**: **KJV**

I suggest to you that it is the angel tongues, not the tongues of men, that are interpreted. These are the two gifts that we have been talking about.

Some Tongues are for a Sign

Tongues are for a sign.

1 Cor 14:22

> [22] WHEREFORE **TONGUES ARE FOR A SIGN**, NOT TO THEM THAT BELIEVE, BUT TO THEM THAT BELIEVE NOT: BUT PROPHESYING SERVETH NOT FOR THEM THAT BELIEVE NOT, BUT FOR THEM WHICH BELIEVE. **KJV**

A stranger who knows that you cannot speak his language will be convicted that the Lord's supernatural power is upon you when you minister to him in his own language.

1 Cor 14:23

> [23] IF THEREFORE THE WHOLE CHURCH BE COME TOGETHER INTO ONE PLACE, AND **ALL SPEAK WITH TONGUES**, AND THERE COME IN THOSE THAT ARE UNLEARNED, OR UNBELIEVERS, WILL THEY NOT SAY THAT YE ARE MAD? **KJV**

If an unbeliever comes into the Church where everybody is talking in the ***tongues of angels***, they will think we are crazy, so those tongues need to be interpreted.

It sounds like Paul in verse 23 is contradicting what he is saying in verse 22, but he is talking about two different kinds of tongues. Paul is talking about one kind of tongues in verse 22 and another kind of tongues in verse 23.

Prophesying in Tongues

1 Cor 14:22

> ²² WHEREFORE **TONGUES ARE FOR A SIGN**, NOT TO THEM THAT BELIEVE, BUT TO THEM THAT BELIEVE NOT: BUT **PROPHESYING SERVETH NOT FOR THEM THAT BELIEVE NOT**, BUT FOR THEM WHICH BELIEVE. **KJV**

Prophecy on the floor of the Church is a prophetic utterance, not prophecy. *Prophecy* is the Word of the Lord coming forth from the Christ in a human being. There is usually no warning, such as a change in voice tone, volume, or inflection. True prophecy must be spiritually discerned because it is spoken in a conversational tone. If you cannot discern it, you will not even know that God is talking to you through that person.

That is the difference between a *prophet* and someone who has the *gift of prophecy*. Everyone who has the gift of prophecy is not a prophet.

A prophet is a person that Christ speaks out of, at His own will. If you are not a believer, you will not be able to recognize when Christ speaks to you through me. If you cannot tell that I stopped talking and Christ started talking, what good is the prophecy going to do you?

Wherefore, prophecy is for the believer who should be able to discern it.

Nevertheless, Paul says in verse 24, if you are in a group function where the whole Church is prophesying, and an unbeliever comes in, he is convinced of all.

1 Cor 14:24

> [24] BUT IF ALL PROPHESY, AND THERE COME IN ONE THAT BELIEVETH NOT, OR ONE UNLEARNED, HE IS CONVINCED OF ALL, HE IS JUDGED OF ALL: **KJV**

That word *convinced* means that *he is understood* of all. This means that everybody who is prophesying can look into the heart of the stranger, and see his need. He is judged of all that he is an unbeliever. Everyone prophesying has discernment as to what his needs are, and what is in his heart . . .

1 Cor 14:25

> [25] AND THUS ARE THE SECRETS OF HIS HEART MADE MANIFEST; AND SO FALLING DOWN ON HIS FACE HE WILL WORSHIP GOD, AND REPORT THAT GOD IS IN YOU OF A TRUTH. **KJV**

. . . so when the gift of prophecy declares openly in the Church that the stranger is a drug addict, or that his heart is broken, for instance, the stranger will be convinced that God is real, and fall down and repent.

It is important to know which kind of tongues the Scripture is talking about, but sometimes it is not so easy to find that out.

A Personal Prayer Language

Here are a few Scriptures to establish that our personal prayer language (not the tongues that we speak out and interpret on the floor of the Church, but the tongues that come out of our mouth when we talk to the Lord, or when we pray), are not a gift.

A prayer language that is not any known, human language, is not a gift in the sense that the gifts are spread across the Church.

Paul said, not everyone prophesies, not everyone heals, not everyone interprets, not everyone speaks in tongues, but a personal prayer language is available to everyone who asks for it.

1 Cor 12:30

> ³⁰ HAVE ALL THE GIFTS OF HEALING? DO ALL SPEAK WITH TONGUES? DO ALL INTERPRET? **KJV**

Therefore, to say, *I do not have a personal prayer language because the gifts are spread throughout the Church, and I just do not have that gift*, is an error. A personal prayer language is not a gift for the Church manifesting through a man, but a blessing for that very man that the tongues are manifesting through. I have three Scriptures to support this statement.

COMMENT: In other words, it is the Devil's lie to make people feel they are not worthy.

PASTOR VITALE: Right, that they may not be worthy, or that they should not seek a personal prayer language because it is not available to everyone, or because some people preach against it.

The Spirit Helps Us Pray

Rom 8:26

> ²⁶ LIKEWISE THE SPIRIT ALSO HELPETH OUR INFIRMITIES: FOR WE KNOW NOT WHAT WE SHOULD PRAY FOR AS WE OUGHT: **BUT THE SPIRIT ITSELF MAKETH**

INTERCESSION FOR US WITH GROANINGS [8]WHICH CANNOT
BE UTTERED.[9] KJV

The word *infirmities* is speaking about spiritual infirmities, not physical infirmities, meaning, everyone that is not standing in full stature is spiritually sick. I am sorry if you do not believe it, but if you cannot measure up to Jesus Christ, who is our standard . . .

Eph 4:13

[13] TILL WE ALL COME IN THE UNITY OF THE FAITH, AND OF THE KNOWLEDGE OF THE SON OF GOD, UNTO A PERFECT MAN, UNTO THE MEASURE OF **THE STATURE OF THE FULNESS OF CHRIST**: KJV

. . . you are spiritually sick, perverted, corrupted and, generally speaking, in pretty bad shape.

So likewise the spirit also helpeth our spiritual weakness, which is manifesting as an inability to communicate with God. We are spiritually weak and crippled in our ability to communicate with God, so we do not know what we should pray for. But the Spirit that is in us *makes intercession for us with groanings which cannot be uttered*.

Here is another witnesses.

---

[8] The Greek word translated, *groanings,* Strong's #4726, simply means *verbal sounds of distress* which are not in any known language.

[9] The Greek word translated, *which cannot be uttered*, Strong's #215, means *sounds that do not express any known language, a prayer language that consists of unintelligible sounds.*

Eph 6:18

> [18] **PRAYING ALWAYS WITH ALL PRAYER AND SUPPLICATION IN THE SPIRIT**, AND WATCHING THEREUNTO WITH ALL PERSEVERANCE AND SUPPLICATION FOR ALL SAINTS; KJV

Praying in the Spirit is part of our armor, which is not a gift.

The last witness is,

Jude 20-21

> [20] BUT YE, BELOVED, BUILDING UP YOURSELVES ON YOUR MOST HOLY FAITH, **PRAYING IN THE HOLY GHOST**,
>
> [21] KEEP YOURSELVES IN THE LOVE OF GOD, LOOKING FOR THE MERCY OF OUR LORD JESUS CHRIST UNTO ETERNAL LIFE. **KJV**

We can pray in the spirit to strengthen Christ in us.

The Spirit Of Anti-Christ

We heard someone preaching against tongues very strongly, a few days ago. Why would anyone come against tongues so strongly when Scripture says,

1 Cor 14:39

> [39] WHEREFORE, BRETHREN, COVET TO PROPHESY, AND **FORBID NOT TO SPEAK WITH TONGUES. KJV**

Any manifestation of the Spirit of God that flows through a human being is glorifying Jesus Christ. It says that Jesus Christ is in that vessel to that potential, whatever it is, and that He will continue on to the fullest extent possible.

78

A false doctrine, or a false prophet, that opposes a true expression of the Holy Spirit from coming forth in any measure, is a spirit of anti-Christ. This does not necessarily mean that everything that the man has to say is anti-Christ, but that could be the case.

God is waiting for the human race to offer up its fallen nature to the Father, who will be all in all. Anti-Christ opposes God's purposes. The whole world lies in wickedness.

The Woman Of Revelation, Chapter 12

The woman in Rev. 12 typifies the personalities of the Church.

Rev 12:1-2

> [1] AND THERE APPEARED A GREAT WONDER IN HEAVEN; **A WOMAN CLOTHED WITH THE SUN, AND THE MOON UNDER HER FEET, AND UPON HER HEAD A CROWN OF TWELVE STARS:**
>
> [2] AND SHE BEING WITH CHILD CRIED, TRAVAILING IN BIRTH, AND PAINED TO BE DELIVERED. **KJV**

After she gives birth to the manchild, which is Christ resurrected in us, she runs into the wilderness.

Rev 12:5-6

> [5] AND **SHE BROUGHT FORTH A MAN CHILD**, WHO WAS TO RULE ALL NATIONS WITH A ROD OF IRON: AND HER CHILD WAS CAUGHT UP UNTO GOD, AND TO HIS THRONE.
>
> [6] AND **THE WOMAN FLED INTO THE WILDERNESS,** WHERE SHE HATH A PLACE PREPARED OF GOD, THAT THEY SHOULD FEED HER THERE A THOUSAND TWO HUNDRED AND THREESCORE DAYS. **KJV**

Mankind is about to be broken into two categories, and actually already has been broken into two groups through Jesus Christ: Those who Christ is appearing in, and those who He is not appearing in.

The Woman giving birth to the manchild signifies mankind, of which we are all a part, about to produce the manchild, but He will be born in only in a few of her members at first. After that, when the First Fruits Company stands up in full stature (when the manchild is born in the First Fruits Company), Satan will go after the rest of the personalities (those who are pregnant with Christ, and those who are not) with a vengeance.

The remainder of the Church, which is not in full stature, will be as vulnerable as a pregnant woman, because the manchild, which is still in utero, is limited in His ability to protect them. Satan knows it would be very, very difficult to overturn the personalities that Christ is already standing in, so she goes after the pregnant personalities with a vengeance.

The Scripture says, ***She flees into the wilderness***. We did a word-by-word study in the Greek and found that the Sons of God deal with her rebellion and pride with education and corrective judgment. After that, she brings her pregnancy to term. Hallelujah!

The Gifts vs. The Reality of Christ

As Christ is formed in you, and you begin to be possessed of His mind, the wisdom of God, and the doctrine of Christ, your spiritual maturity diminishes the gifts and you speak in tongues and prophesy less and less.

A gift from God can be a severe stumbling block if you have not matured enough to overcome your pride. Pride always wants to exalt itself because of the gifts that you did not do anything to deserve, and reluctance to let the gifts go works against your own spiritual maturation.

In Acts 9:17, Paul receives the Holy Ghost, his spiritual sight, and is filled with the Holy Ghost.

Acts 9:17

> [17] AND ANANIAS WENT HIS WAY, AND ENTERED INTO THE HOUSE; AND PUTTING HIS HANDS ON HIM SAID, BROTHER SAUL, THE LORD, EVEN JESUS, THAT APPEARED UNTO THEE IN THE WAY AS THOU CAMEST, HATH SENT ME, THAT **THOU MIGHTEST RECEIVE THY SIGHT, AND BE FILLED WITH THE HOLY GHOST. KJV**

Earlier, I quoted Acts 1:5, where Jesus said to the apostles, *In a few days you will be baptized with the Holy Ghost*, and, after that, they were *filled with* the Holy Ghost. So, we now know that *baptism* with the Holy Ghost is the same as being *filled* with the Holy Ghost.

The word *Baptism* signifies the *action* of the Holy Ghost, and the words *filled with* signify the *effect* that the Holy Ghost had upon the apostles.

Baptized with the Holy Ghost is the same thing as *filled with the Holy Ghost*, but both *baptized* and *filled* are different than *receiving* the Holy Ghost.

RESURRECTION

Perfection (Full Stature)

In Acts 9:17, we see Jesus appearing to Paul as a ball of light, and instructing Paul, who was blinded by the encounter, to sit in darkness until a disciple named Ananias came to lay hands on him.

Acts 9:17-18

> [17] AND ANANIAS WENT HIS WAY, AND ENTERED INTO THE HOUSE; AND PUTTING HIS HANDS ON HIM SAID, BROTHER SAUL, THE LORD, EVEN JESUS, THAT APPEARED UNTO THEE IN THE WAY AS THOU CAMEST, HATH SENT ME, THAT THOU MIGHTEST **RECEIVE THY SIGHT, AND BE FILLED WITH THE HOLY GHOST**.

> [18] AND IMMEDIATELY THERE FELL FROM HIS EYES AS IT HAD BEEN SCALES: AND HE RECEIVED SIGHT FORTHWITH, AND AROSE, AND WAS BAPTIZED. **KJV**

Three things happened to Paul which, I suggest to you, were spiritual, as well as physical. I do not doubt that Paul's physical sight was restored, that he rose up (which means his sighted life was restored), and that he was filled with the Holy Ghost. But I also believe that Paul was baptized in the Name of the Lord Jesus and that Adam rose from the dead in him and gave him spiritual sight, or *spiritual understanding*. This means that Paul ascended into perfection, or full stature.

Eph 4:13

> [13] TILL WE ALL COME IN THE UNITY OF THE FAITH, AND OF THE KNOWLEDGE OF THE SON OF GOD, UNTO A PERFECT MAN, **UNTO THE MEASURE OF THE STATURE OF THE FULNESS OF CHRIST**: **KJV**

The Resurrection Of Christ

Luke 24:46

> [46] AND SAID UNTO THEM, THUS IT IS WRITTEN, AND THUS IT BEHOVED CHRIST TO SUFFER, AND TO **RISE FROM THE DEAD THE THIRD DAY**: **KJV**

The article, *the*, which is in the Greek text, but not translated, tells us that Lk 24:46 is speaking about *Jesus, the Christ* . . . .

1 Cor 15:3-4

> [3] FOR I DELIVERED UNTO YOU FIRST OF ALL THAT WHICH I ALSO RECEIVED, HOW **THAT CHRIST** DIED FOR OUR SINS ACCORDING TO THE SCRIPTURES;
>
> [4] AND THAT HE WAS BURIED, AND THAT HE ROSE AGAIN THE THIRD DAY ACCORDING TO THE SCRIPTURES: **KJV**

. . . . But, the article, *the*, does not appear before the word, *Christ*, in 1 Cor. 14:3-4.

Luke 24:46 is speaking about *Jesus of Nazareth*, who was *the Christ in the days of his flesh*, rising from the dead, but 1 Cor. 15:3-4, is speaking about *Adam, the Christ of the previous age*, resurrected in the man, Jesus of Nazareth.

All of humanity is descended from Adam, whose death resulted in this present existence. *Christ* is the name Adam is called by when he is resurrected in a fallen man (1 Cor. 15:22), and, so, it was Adam who spoke through the man, Jesus, saying,

John 8:58

> [58] JESUS SAID UNTO THEM, VERILY, VERILY, I SAY UNTO YOU, **BEFORE ABRAHAM WAS, I AM. KJV**

. . . meaning, *I existed before Abraham did.*

1 Cor 15:22

> [22] FOR AS **IN ADAM ALL DIE**, EVEN SO IN CHRIST SHALL ALL BE MADE ALIVE. **KJV**

Adam, the living soul, died to his immortality, and, as a consequence, all of his descendants are born as spiritually dead, mortal men. But when Adam, who is the immortal Christ of the age of innocence, is resurrected in a mortal descendant of Adam, that man who is dead because of sin, is made alive.

Adam was overthrown and died to his immortality in the previous age because of sin, and his spirit, Jehovah's breath, was buried underneath the earth of the physical bodies of humanity. But Adam rose from the dead in the man, Jesus . . . .

Rev 1:5

> [5] AND FROM JESUS CHRIST, WHO IS THE FAITHFUL WITNESS, AND **THE FIRST BEGOTTEN OF THE DEAD**, AND THE PRINCE OF THE KINGS OF THE EARTH. UNTO HIM THAT LOVED US, AND WASHED US FROM OUR SINS IN HIS OWN BLOOD, **KJV**

The Third Day

The Interlinear text says, He rose again *the day the third*.

The word, *third*, speaks about the third part of man, his negative principle, Satan.

Adam, *the* star . . .

Gen 1:16

> [16] AND GOD MADE TWO GREAT LIGHTS; THE GREATER LIGHT TO RULE THE DAY, AND THE LESSER LIGHT TO RULE THE NIGHT: **HE MADE THE STARS ALSO. KJV**

. . . of Elohim's *Day*,

Gen 1:5

> [5] AND GOD CALLED THE LIGHT **DAY**, AND THE DARKNESS HE CALLED NIGHT. AND THE EVENING AND THE MORNING WERE THE FIRST DAY. **KJV**

. . . rose from the dead out of *the carnal mind* that the man, Jesus, inherited from his mother.

2 Peter 1:19

> [19] WE HAVE ALSO A MORE SURE WORD OF PROPHECY; WHEREUNTO YE DO WELL THAT YE TAKE HEED, AS UNTO A LIGHT THAT SHINETH IN A DARK PLACE, UNTIL THE DAY DAWN, AND **THE DAY STAR ARISE IN YOUR HEARTS: KJV**

. . . and,

1 Cor 15:5

> [5] AND THAT HE **WAS SEEN OF CEPHAS**, THEN OF THE TWELVE: **KJV**

Peter is included in the twelve, so why would Jesus refer to Peter twice, once as *Cephas* and a second time as one of the twelve?

Why would Paul say *Cephas*, instead of *Peter*, when Jesus addressed Peter as Cephas only once, in John 1:42, and that was *before* His crucifixion?

Cephas means *stone*, which can mean the hard covering over the seed of many fruits.

John 1:42

> [42] AND HE BROUGHT HIM TO JESUS. AND WHEN JESUS BEHELD HIM, HE SAID, THOU ART SIMON THE SON OF JONA: **THOU SHALT BE CALLED CEPHAS, WHICH IS BY INTERPRETATION, A STONE. KJV**

Also, how could there have been 12, since there were only *eleven* disciples when the man, Jesus, was resurrected, Judas being already dead.

If the resurrection spoken about in 1 Cor 15:5 was the physical resurrection of the man, Jesus of Nazareth, if that were the case, Judas would have already hanged himself.

Mark 16:14

> [14] AFTERWARD HE APPEARED UNTO **THE ELEVEN** AS THEY SAT AT MEAT, AND UPBRAIDED THEM WITH THEIR UNBELIEF AND HARDNESS OF HEART, BECAUSE THEY BELIEVED NOT THEM WHICH HAD SEEN HIM AFTER HE WAS RISEN. **KJV**

There were only *eleven* disciples when the man, Jesus, was resurrected, Judas being dead.

The Greek word translated *he was seen*, Strong's #3700, can also be translated *to appear*.

Also, the number *twelve* could not be talking about the disciples, because they were only *eleven*. But the number twelve can signify the heart center . . . .

I suggest to you that Paul said *Cephas*, because he was speaking about the appearance of *Christ*, the First Fruits . . .

1 Cor 15:20

> [20] BUT NOW IS CHRIST RISEN FROM THE DEAD, AND
> BECOME **THE FIRSTFRUITS OF THEM THAT SLEPT. KJV**

. . . the resurrected Adam (called *Christ* when appearing in a man) , who rose from the dead and appeared in **the heart center** (twelve) of *the man, Jesus*, BEFORE *the MAN, Jesus rose from the dead,*

The Resurrection Of Jesus

The point is, that if Adam had not risen in the man, Jesus, **BEFORE** the man, Jesus, was crucified, the man, Jesus, would not have risen from the dead.

In other words, it was the presence of Adam, the living soul, the resurrected Christ of the previous age *within Jesus*, that raised him from the dead by the power of the Father. This truth accounts for the two angels at Jesus' tomb,

John 20:12

> [12] AND SEETH **TWO ANGELS** IN WHITE SITTING, THE
> ONE AT THE HEAD, AND THE OTHER AT THE FEET, WHERE THE
> BODY OF JESUS HAD LAIN. **KJV**

One angel was Jesus' soul and the other was the resurrected Christ. There were two angels because the soul of Jesus was not yet blended with the resurrected Christ into one glorified man . . .

John 20:17

> [17] JESUS SAITH UNTO HER, **TOUCH ME NOT; FOR I
> AM NOT YET ASCENDED TO MY FATHER**: BUT GO TO MY
> BRETHREN, AND SAY UNTO THEM, I ASCEND UNTO MY
> FATHER, AND YOUR FATHER; AND TO MY GOD, AND YOUR
> GOD. **KJV**

So, if Adam (called *Christ* when resurrected in a man) did not rise in the man, Jesus . . .

1 Cor 15:14

> [14] AND **IF CHRIST BE NOT RISEN**, THEN IS OUR
> PREACHING VAIN, AND YOUR FAITH IS ALSO VAIN. **KJV**

. . . then we have no hope that he will rise in us . . .

1 Cor 15:18-20

> [18] THEN **THEY ALSO WHICH ARE FALLEN ASLEEP**
> IN CHRIST ARE PERISHED.

> [19] IF IN THIS LIFE ONLY WE HAVE HOPE IN CHRIST,
> WE ARE OF ALL MEN MOST MISERABLE.

. . . if he did not rise in Jesus, the first fruits of them that slept.

> [20] BUT NOW IS CHRIST RISEN FROM THE DEAD, AND BECOME **THE FIRSTFRUITS OF THEM THAT SLEPT. KJV**

Gen 2:21

> [21] AND **THE LORD GOD CAUSED A DEEP SLEEP TO FALL UPON ADAM** AND HE SLEPT: AND HE TOOK ONE OF HIS RIBS, AND CLOSED UP THE FLESH INSTEAD THEREOF; **KJV**

Now, if Jesus was the first one of those who slept to rise, He had to be sleeping at some point. So, since the word *sleeping* means the death of this existence, Jesus could not have been perfect at birth.

Now, if Jesus was not perfect at birth, how could He be the Son of God, except that Adam, the Son of God, rose from the dead in Him?

Luke 3:38

> [38] WHICH WAS THE SON OF ENOS, WHICH WAS THE SON OF SETH, WHICH WAS **THE SON OF ADAM, WHICH WAS THE SON OF GOD. KJV**

Adam is the Son of God, and the Lord Jesus Christ is Savior. The word, *Son*, signifies Adam's relationship to the one above him, that is, God; and *Savior*, signifies Jesus' relationship to the one beneath Him, that is, mankind -- but the resurrected Adam and the resurrected Jesus, became one new man . . .

Eph 2:15

> [15] HAVING ABOLISHED IN HIS FLESH THE ENMITY, EVEN THE LAW OF COMMANDMENTS CONTAINED IN ORDINANCES; FOR TO MAKE IN HIMSELF **OF TWAIN ONE NEW MAN,** SO MAKING PEACE; **KJV**

. . . when the man, Jesus, was glorified.

The Lord Jesus Christ, who is now both the Son of God (Adam) and Savior of mankind, . . .

Mark 1:1

[1] THE BEGINNING OF THE GOSPEL OF **JESUS CHRIST, THE SON OF GOD**; **KJV**

Titus 3:6

[6] WHICH HE SHED ON US ABUNDANTLY THROUGH **JESUS CHRIST OUR SAVIOUR**; **KJV**

. . . is saving mankind from death by raising Christ from the dead in each of us.

Paul received the life of the Lord Jesus Christ, and Christ began to rise from the dead within him. Christ within Paul baptized, or filled him with the Holy Ghost, and Paul became an apostle of the glorified Jesus with spiritual sight. Paul was the first mortal man after Jesus to experience the resurrection from the dead with full power and authority.

- *Receiving* the Holy Ghost does not imply that you have been raised from the dead.

- **To be filled with the Holy Ghost,** to be totally *filled up*, implies that your human spirit has been completed.

- Your life has been joined to you. Your righteousness has been joined to you.

- **We are complete in Christ Jesus.** He is our righteousness; He is our life; He is our faith.

- *Filled up* with the Holy Ghost does not necessarily mean full stature, because it is possible to be *temporarily* filled up with the Holy Ghost. That is, the Holy Ghost can rise within a man and bring him to a condition of full stature, but then recede, as

91

water washing over a man recedes, after His purpose is accomplished.

The Gospel Is Not Simple

I cannot tell you how many people have said to me, ***The gospel is simple, why are you preaching this complicated message***? The gospel is not simple. That is a lie. The gospel is very complicated. People study the Scripture all their lives and do not know the whole message. What a lie, to say it is simple.

2 Cor 11:3

> [3] BUT I FEAR, LEST BY ANY MEANS, AS THE SERPENT BEGUILED EVE THROUGH HIS SUBTILTY, SO YOUR MINDS SHOULD BE CORRUPTED FROM **THE SIMPLICITY THAT IS IN CHRIST**. **KJV**

The Greek word translated, ***simplicity***, actually means ***single***. This Scripture is talking about keeping your eyes on Christ, so that you do not live out of two minds.

Jesus talked in parables so that only the elect would hear and understand. But when He tried to explain His experience on the Mount of Transfiguration to Peter, James and John, His inner circle . . .

Matt 17:2

> [2] AND **WAS TRANSFIGURED BEFORE THEM:** AND HIS FACE DID SHINE AS THE SUN, AND HIS RAIMENT WAS WHITE AS THE LIGHT. **KJV**

. . even they did not know what He was talking about.

The gospel is not simple. It is very difficult, and you must study to show yourself approved. It is a life's work, and even then, knowledge is only in part.

BAPTISM INTO CHRIST (FIRE)

Now, we come to *the Baptism into Christ*, which is sometimes also known as the *Baptism with Fire*.

Matt 3:11

> [11] I INDEED BAPTIZE YOU WITH WATER UNTO REPENTANCE: BUT HE THAT COMETH AFTER ME IS MIGHTIER THAN I, WHOSE SHOES I AM NOT WORTHY TO BEAR: HE SHALL **BAPTIZE YOU WITH THE HOLY GHOST, AND WITH FIRE**: **KJV**

We know that Christ is the Lake of Fire.

Heb 12:29

> [29] FOR OUR **GOD IS A CONSUMING FIRE**. **KJV**

Christ is our righteousness.

1 Cor 1:30

> [30] BUT OF HIM ARE YE IN **CHRIST JESUS**, WHO OF GOD **IS MADE UNTO US WISDOM, AND RIGHTEOUSNESS**, AND SANCTIFICATION, AND REDEMPTION: **KJV**

Christ is fire, so the Baptism with Fire is the Baptism into Christ.

The reality of *the Baptism into Christ* is that all of the parts of fallen Adam, our Old Man, Satan (unconscious mind), Leviathan (subconscious mind), Cain (conscious mind), are being cast into

95

the Lake of Fire, which is Christ in you, your only hope that you will be glorified.

Col 1:27

> [27] To whom God would make known what is the riches of the glory of this mystery among the Gentiles; which is **Christ in you, the hope of glory**: **KJV**

Your fallen nature must *spiritually* burn up for you to be glorified . . .

2 Peter 3:10

> [10] But the day of the Lord will come as a thief in the night; in the which the heavens shall pass away with a great noise, and **the elements shall melt with fervent heat**, the earth also and the works that are therein shall be burned up. **KJV**

. . . because the spiritual fire that judges the hidden sins of our heart, purifies us. Our New Man, The part of us that survives, will live on in a new form which will submit to Christ.

The Baptism into Christ, which is the Baptism with Fire, is the end of the several stages of Baptism. There is only one Baptism, with many stages thereof, and that is into Christ. When the testing becomes so strong that you feel like you are burning, you will know that you are experiencing the final stages of the Baptism into Christ.

If you do not understand the Baptism with Fire, you may feel guilty, thinking that you did something wrong. I believe that as we near the season in which we will be entering into full stature, people will pass through the Baptism with Fire much more quickly.

I have been in that stage for years now, but the fire just keeps increasing. Maybe the people who are in the garden at midnight will go through it faster. I am at the point now where I pray continuously for this baptism with fire to be completed. I feel like I am in the *transition* stage of childbirth that a woman experiences just before her baby is born. Just let it happen already. I hope it is not too much longer.

Mark 16:16

> [16] HE THAT BELIEVETH AND IS BAPTIZED SHALL BE SAVED; BUT HE THAT BELIEVETH NOT SHALL BE DAMNED. KJV

He who believes what? He who believes *the Gospel of Perfection* will be baptized in the Name of the Lord Jesus. *To be perfect* means *to be complete.*

Matt 5:48

> [48] BE YE THEREFORE PERFECT, EVEN AS YOUR FATHER WHICH IS IN HEAVEN IS PERFECT. KJV

He who believes (the Gospel of Perfection – that it is possible in Christ Jesus to become perfect), *and is baptized,* or *filled, with the Holy Ghost, shall be saved*.

Baptism, or permanent, full immersion into Christ, is full salvation, spirit, soul and body.

When you believe that it is possible for Jesus to complete (fill) you, you will be baptized in the Name of the Lord Jesus (which baptism imparts the seed of Christ that the Holy Ghost carries), and Christ shall immerse (baptize) your fallen nature in the lake of fire, and you shall be saved,

But, whoever does not believe that Jesus can complete him, shall continue to have their motives and behavior judged by Satan, the enforcer of the Sowing & Reaping Judgment.

> ***Mark 16:16 – AT:*** *Whoever believes that it is possible for Jesus to complete them shall be baptized in the Name of the Lord Jesus, which baptism imparts the seed of Christ that the Holy Ghost carries, and Christ shall immerse your fallen nature in the lake of fire, and you shall be saved,*
>
> *But, whoever does not believe that Jesus can complete him, shall continue to have their motives and behavior judged by Satan, the enforcer of the Sowing & Reaping Judgment. **(ATB)***

Salvation Is A Process

QUESTION: What does that Scripture, ***Work out your salvation with fear and trembling,*** mean?

PASTOR VITALE: It means we are ***in the process of*** being saved. As soon as we profess faith in Jesus Christ as our savior, we receive ***the promise of salvation, and*** our spirit is saved right away. Peter calls the salvation of our spirit, ***the common salvation*[10]** . . .

Jude 3

> [3] BELOVED, WHEN I GAVE ALL DILIGENCE TO WRITE UNTO YOU OF **THE COMMON SALVATION,** IT WAS NEEDFUL FOR ME TO WRITE UNTO YOU, AND EXHORT YOU THAT YE SHOULD EARNESTLY CONTEND FOR THE FAITH WHICH WAS ONCE DELIVERED UNTO THE SAINTS. **KJV**

. . . but the salvation of our soul requires a warfare.

---

[10] See, ***The Common Salvation*** (Sheila R. Vitale, Christ-Centered Kabbalah, Pub Long Island, NY, June 2014).

2 Cor 10:4

> [4] (FOR THE WEAPONS OF OUR WARFARE ARE NOT CARNAL, BUT MIGHTY THROUGH GOD TO THE PULLING DOWN OF STRONG HOLDS;) **KJV**

Weapons are delivered to us means that we have received the ability to be saved, but we must do the spiritual work of salvation.

James 2:17

> [17] EVEN SO F<u>AITH, IF IT HATH NOT WORKS, IS DEAD</u>, BEING ALONE. **KJV**

John 9:4

> [4] I MUST **WORK** THE WORKS OF HIM THAT SENT ME, **WHILE IT IS DAY**: THE NIGHT COMETH, WHEN NO MAN CAN WORK. **KJV**

If the Church knew that only our spirit is saved initially, they would be spending more time looking inward to deal with their own sins, and less time trying to save everyone else. The Scripture clearly teaches the on-going purging of the conscience,

1 Peter 5:8

> [8] **BE SOBER, BE VIGILANT**; BECAUSE YOUR ADVERSARY THE DEVIL, AS A ROARING LION, WALKETH ABOUT, SEEKING WHOM HE MAY DEVOUR: **KJV**

We do not burn in hell forever if we die. Eternal punishment for a finite crime opposes the Scriptural principle of *an eye for an eye and a tooth for a tooth.* Man is mortal, and his *ability to sin* ends with the death of the body. We would have to continue to sin for eternity to justify eternal punishment.

If you have the opportunity to be found in Christ when He appears, and this is the hour of appearing, would you not want it?

The Scripture says that when Christ stands up, there will be wailing and gnashing of teeth. Many will feel bad, like fools, when they realize that they chose the dung of this world over the reality.

1 Peter 1:9

> [9] RECEIVING THE END OF YOUR FAITH, EVEN THE SALVATION OF YOUR SOULS. **KJV**

Our soul is in the process of being saved. Salvation is purification. No sin will enter into the Kingdom of Heaven. Our carnal mind must be purified and brought into total submission to the Christ within us, which is what the Baptism into Christ accomplishes. We will pick up our carnal mind by the strength of Christ within us, and throw her into the Lake of Fire, which is Christ Jesus.

People do not want to hear this, but it does not matter whether you drink, shoot up drugs, engage in illicit sex, or eat to deal with your anxiety. All of those activities are idolatrous if you are engaging in them compulsively, but some are obviously more destructive than others.

Even in marriage, it is idolatry for a man to desire sex with his wife *only* because he had a bad day and wants to feel good. It is the truth. Anything other than Christ that satisfies you or calms you, is the operation of your sin nature. ***The sex act should be an exchange of mutual affection.***

Paul said that he had total authority over his body. There is nothing wrong with eating Chinese duck, but when you eat duck because you are upset, instead of turning to Jesus, there is something wrong with that.

Paul said all things were legal for him, but all things were not expedient. We are supposed to have total control over our lives. Of course, nobody is there yet, but it is good to see progress in these areas.

Baptism into His Death

The Baptism into Christ is in two parts. The first part is Baptism into His death, and the second part is Baptism into His life, or His resurrection.

Rom 6:3-9

> [3] KNOW YE NOT, THAT SO MANY OF US AS WERE BAPTIZED INTO JESUS CHRIST WERE **BAPTIZED INTO HIS DEATH?**
>
> [4] THEREFORE **WE ARE BURIED WITH HIM BY BAPTISM INTO DEATH:** THAT LIKE AS CHRIST WAS RAISED UP FROM THE DEAD BY THE GLORY OF THE FATHER, EVEN SO WE ALSO SHOULD WALK IN NEWNESS OF LIFE.
>
> [5] FOR IF WE HAVE BEEN PLANTED TOGETHER **IN THE LIKENESS OF HIS DEATH,** WE SHALL BE ALSO IN THE LIKENESS OF HIS RESURRECTION:
>
> [6] KNOWING THIS, THAT OUR **OLD MAN IS CRUCIFIED WITH HIM, THAT THE BODY OF SIN MIGHT BE DESTROYED,** THAT HENCEFORTH WE SHOULD NOT SERVE SIN.
>
> [7] FOR **HE THAT IS DEAD IS FREED FROM SIN.**
>
> [8] NOW **IF WE BE DEAD WITH CHRIST,** WE BELIEVE THAT WE SHALL ALSO LIVE WITH HIM:
>
> [9] KNOWING THAT CHRIST BEING RAISED FROM THE DEAD DIETH NO MORE; **DEATH HATH NO MORE DOMINION OVER HIM. KJV**

God created only one living soul, and we are all individual members of that living soul. We can count our carnal mind as slain from the moment that Christ begins to be formed in us, because it is only a matter of time until He slays the enmity in our flesh.

Christ is alive and living freely in us, but as of this time, Jesus of Nazareth is the only member of the living soul who succeeded in slaying his carnal mind.

When Christ is formed in us, He begins to save our soul . . .

Heb 6:19

> [19] WHICH HOPE WE HAVE AS **AN ANCHOR OF THE SOUL**, BOTH SURE AND STEDFAST, AND WHICH ENTERETH INTO THAT WITHIN THE VEIL; **KJV**

. . . which means that the that emerging Christ within us begins to slay our carnal mind.

Look at it this way, there are two groups of human beings in the world today.

The carnal mind is ruling and reigning and living her life through one group of human beings. No man is strong enough to restrain *Leviathan,* the subconscious part of our carnal mind. The Scripture says that no one can approach him.

Job 41:10

> [10] NONE IS SO FIERCE THAT DARE STIR HIM UP: WHO THEN IS ABLE TO STAND BEFORE ME? **KJV**

Christ, the second group of human beings, is approaching Leviathan with the strength of God.

Right now, there is only one person in that second group of human beings who has fully slain his carnal mind, and that is Jesus Christ of Nazareth.

Rom 1:4

> ⁴ AND DECLARED TO BE THE SON OF GOD WITH POWER, ACCORDING TO THE SPIRIT OF HOLINESS, **BY THE RESURRECTION FROM THE DEAD**: **KJV**

From the moment Christ begins to be formed in you, you are in the second group of people who have the strength in Christ to slay your carnal mind. There is someone in you who can approach your carnal mind, and not only can Christ approach Leviathan, He fully intends to slay her.

The Scripture that says, *we are baptized unto His death*, means that you have moved into the second category and that your carnal mind is dying, and shall, eventually, fully die.

You are baptized into Jesus' death when Christ begins to be formed in you, and you become that part of humanity whose carnal mind is being killed. Likewise, of course, as your carnal mind is being killed, you are baptized into the Lord Jesus, and you become filled up with His life.

1 Cor 15:29

> ²⁹ ELSE WHAT SHALL THEY DO WHICH ARE BAPTIZED FOR THE DEAD, **IF THE DEAD RISE NOT AT ALL?** **WHY ARE THEY THEN BAPTIZED FOR THE DEAD?** **KJV**

We are in a hopeless condition if Adam, who died when time began, is not raised from the dead in us. Why do we go through this painful, spiritual crucifixion of our carnal mind if Christ is not being raised from the dead in us? We must be a baptized into the death of *the Son of God*, if *the Son of Man* is to rise from the dead in us.

John 12:34

> ³⁴ THE PEOPLE ANSWERED HIM, WE HAVE HEARD
> OUT OF THE LAW THAT **CHRIST ABIDETH FOR EVER**: AND
> HOW SAYEST THOU, THE SON OF MAN MUST BE LIFTED UP?
> WHO IS THIS SON OF MAN? **KJV**

These are reciprocal events which we experience simultaneously. Adam rose from the dead first in the man, Jesus, and now our carnal mind dies as Jesus life is imparted to us by His glorified Spirit.

Jesus is the first mortal man to ascend out of the death of the carnal mind that He inherited from his parents, to be born again into Elohim's visible, spiritual world above the sea of the soul realm. For this reason, Jesus shall always have the preeminence over all of the Sons of God who ascend out of their carnal mind, and are glorified.

Heb 2:10

> ¹⁰ FOR IT BECAME HIM, FOR WHOM ARE ALL THINGS,
> AND BY WHOM ARE ALL THINGS, IN **BRINGING MANY SONS
> UNTO GLORY**, TO MAKE THE CAPTAIN OF THEIR SALVATION
> PERFECT THROUGH SUFFERINGS. **KJV**

Why? Because Christ, the Savior, raised from the dead in the midst of mortal man, is still in the fallen world underneath the firmament. The glorified Jesus Christ is His only connection to the world above. Wherefore, the maturing Christ must marry Jesus, who is above.

Christ in the earth of an individual, married to Jesus who is above, is called ***Christ Jesus***.

Some people experience Christ Jesus taking over their carnal mind temporarily, for a specific purpose that the Lord wants to accomplish. But when Christ Jesus overlays our carnal mind ***PERMANENTLY***, we shall have the strength to overcome Satan, the unconscious part of our carnal mind, Leviathan, the subconscious part of our carnal mind; and Cain, the conscious part of our carnal mind, and we shall rise into eternal life in Christ Jesus.

This understanding should give you hope as you go through the painful experiences of your personal tribulation. Everybody has his/her own testimony.

Whatever pain you might experience, the hope of Christ appearing in you and marrying Jesus above, is not for naught. Christ Jesus shall defeat the powers and principalities that rule this world, which continuously subject us to death and hell. There is no other way to leave this world, other than physical death. *AND WE ARE HERE BECAUSE OF OUR SIN.*

Baptism into His Resurrection

The Foolishness of Preaching

COMMENT: Does the carnal mind begin to die when we understand what you are saying?

PASTOR VITALE: Your carnal mind begins to die when the Holy Spirit joins to your human spirit and Christ begins to be formed in you. It is Christ in you who understands the message.

This is not my message. The Lord Jesus is bringing this message and the anointing that is falling through me, for the specific purpose of penetrating your human spirit and grafting Christ to you.

COMMENT: But how does that take place? By listening to the message and understanding it?

PASTOR VITALE: By the foolishness of preaching, which is more than listening. Jesus said . . .

105

John 6:63

> [63] IT IS THE SPIRIT THAT QUICKENETH; THE FLESH PROFITETH NOTHING: **THE WORDS THAT I SPEAK UNTO YOU, THEY ARE SPIRIT, AND THEY ARE LIFE. KJV**

. . . meaning, words preached under the anointing are penetrating, spiritual sperm to those who open themselves up to Him.

The message would not do you any good if you were sitting here with your heart plugged up, but since you are willing to understand to the fullest extent that the Lord will let you, He who is Spirit, is penetrating your soul and fertilizing your potential to birth Christ.

Spiritual Reproduction

In human sexual reproduction, there are thousands, if not millions, of sperm that flow over a female egg before it is fertilized. Each individual is unique as to how many messages one would have to hear, or be subjected to, to conceive Christ. Of course, once fertilization has taken place, the same words become the spiritual food that nourishes the emerging Christ in you.

I do not want anyone to think that they can conceive Christ by sitting under this anointing one time. You stay under the anointing for a season, however long that season may be, until the Lord Jesus releases you. I do not want you here any longer than Christ calls you to be here, but neither do I want anyone to think that He has called you here for only one or two meetings. That is highly unlikely.

The Engrafted Word

Some people think that they only have to listen to the message, but God wants you to understand that there is much more to conceiving Christ than that. You are being penetrated by these words. James speaks about the ***engrafted Word***.

James 1:21

> [21] WHEREFORE LAY APART ALL FILTHINESS AND SUPERFLUITY OF NAUGHTINESS, AND RECEIVE WITH MEEKNESS **THE ENGRAFTED WORD,** WHICH IS ABLE TO SAVE YOUR SOULS. **KJV**

The Word, which is Spirit and life, has to get inside of your mind and root there to reproduce the Spirit of the man who is preaching by the Spirit of Christ in you. The time and effort you put into listening to messages will have been in vain, even if you have been sitting here for six years, if the Spirit that is preaching through the preacher does not start to grow in you.

An intellectual knowledge of this Word will bring nothing but death. The Word must be formed in you, reproduced in you. Christ, who is speaking through the preacher, must be reproduced in your mind.

The Lord Jesus is raising up preachers right now for the revival that is coming. Many will be needed to preach the Gospel of Perfection. One person cannot possibly do the job. Even ten people cannot do the job. The whole world has to hear this message, but the Lord Jesus will start with one group.

Let us say, hypothetically, that it is our group. When the Christ within each of us matures to the point that He can teach the Gospel of Perfection, each of us will have disciples, who will eventually have disciples, who will eventually have disciples, etc. In this way, the Gospel of Perfection will expand throughout humanity. If there are more groups like this across the world, then the Gospel of Perfection is already spreading out into the four corners of the earth.

COMMENT: It is going to take time, because it is taking time to get the Gospel of Perfection across to us.

PASTOR VITALE: I think that once the First Fruits stand up in full stature, ascending into perfection will be easier and faster for those following. I am not in full stature. I believe that if Paul or Peter were standing here, they might be able to help you step up with only a few meetings, or even, possibly, with a one-time encounter. You might have heard me preach that this is what Peter was doing for Ananias. [11]

Gold and Silver Have I None

I believe there is a double (physical and spiritual) meaning to the Scripture that talks about Peter's encounter with the man who was begging at the gate. Peter said, ***Gold and silver have I none, but in the name of Jesus Christ of Nazareth stand up and walk* . . .**

Acts 3:6

> [6] THEN PETER SAID, **SILVER AND GOLD HAVE I NONE**; BUT SUCH AS **I HAVE** GIVE **I** THEE: IN THE NAME OF JESUS CHRIST OF NAZARETH RISE UP **AND** WALK. **KJV**

. . . and the man's ankles were strengthened, and he jumped up and leaped.

Acts 3:7-8

> [7] AND HE TOOK HIM BY THE RIGHT HAND, AND LIFTED HIM UP: AND IMMEDIATELY HIS FEET AND ANKLE BONES RECEIVED STRENGTH.

-----

[11] See, ***Ananais & Sapphira***, LEM Message # 386 and ***Sofia, Wisdom (Ananais & Sapphira)***, CCK Message # 838.

> [8] AND **HE LEAPING UP STOOD, AND WALKED,** AND
> ENTERED WITH THEM INTO THE TEMPLE, WALKING, AND
> LEAPING, AND PRAISING GOD. **KJV**

I believe that not only were the man's physical ankles strengthened, but that the high spiritual authority that Peter spoke with, caught the man up into Christ Jesus.

The Interlinear Text of *Acts, Chapter 3*, indicates that the man recognized Peter and John. An untranslated word[12] reveals that the man was not begging for money, but asking for a spiritual awakening.

Acts 3:2

> [2] AND A CERTAIN MAN LAME FROM HIS MOTHER'S
> WOMB WAS CARRIED, WHOM THEY LAID DAILY AT THE GATE
> OF THE TEMPLE WHICH IS CALLED BEAUTIFUL, **TO ASK ALMS**
> **OF THEM THAT ENTERED INTO THE TEMPLE;** **KJV**

Verse 2 of *The Interlinear Text* indicates that the man had heard Peter and John preach and welcomed the spiritual, virile seed which was deposited at the door of his mind.

The eye contact between them (verses 4-5) confirmed to Peter that the man believed the Word, steadfastly expecting a miracle . . .

Acts 3:4-5

> [4] AND PETER, **FASTENING HIS EYES UPON HIM** WITH
> JOHN, SAID, LOOK ON US.

---

[12]   Strong's #2983, to give a person access to himself, to receive what is offered.

⁵ AND HE GAVE HEED UNTO THEM, EXPECTING TO
RECEIVE SOMETHING OF THEM. **KJV**

... and Peter said in verse 6 quoted above, I give you what I have, let Christ (silver/salvation) begin to come forth in you[13] [and be joined to] Jesus (gold), who is above Satan,[14] and wake up [out of death] and live in the Spirit of Jesus Christ of Nazareth.

I am not in full stature, so it is taking a long time for Christ to be raised in the people I teach. It is hard on you, and it is hard on me.

The Body Of Christ

We are not this physical body, and we are not this carnal mind. We are our personality, which is soul. When our human spirit escapes from our carnal mind, we [our personality/soul] will flee into, and become one with, Christ Jesus, the Lake of Fire. Then, He will overshadow our carnal mind and swallow up the vile elements of our old nature.

Our physical body is solid, but our new, glorified, body is an ethereal body. It is a celestial body. You can see through it. When Jesus walked on the water His disciples thought He was a ghost, because He was walking in His celestial body.

---

[13]   The words ***begin to come forth in you***, are a translation of the Greek word translated ***have, Strong's*** 5225.

[14]   Satan is a translation of the Greek word translated ***none,*** a negative particle. By translator's license, all negative particles can be translated as any negative principle of the Scripture.

1 Cor 12:13

> ¹³ FOR BY ONE SPIRIT ARE WE ALL
> BAPTIZED INTO **ONE BODY**, ... **KJV**

What body? The body of Christ. What is the body of Christ? The body of Christ exists in the lower and the upper heaven at the same time.

The *lower heaven* is the spiritual dimension of this physical world, which appeared underneath the firmament after Adam died and fell down into this world. The *upper heaven* is the spiritual world above the firmament, which is revealed to humanity through the Lord Jesus Christ.

The body of Christ in the *lower heaven* consists of the personalities (souls) who are living out of the resurrected Christ within themselves. The body of Christ in the *upper heaven* consists of the personalities who ascend into the spiritual world above because they prefer Christ to this world. They are joined to Jesus who is above, because they have rejected their carnal mind.

Christ Jesus is divided from Himself in the lower heaven, because His many personalities (bodies) are living, at least partially, out of their carnal mind.

Let us say that the moon signifies the personality (body), and that Christ Jesus signifies the sun. We can say, then, that the personality (body) which is in perfect submission to Christ Jesus, the sun, is totally eclipsed by Him. This does not mean that the personality ceases to exist as an individual but, on the contrary, becomes a perfect, individual expression of Christ Jesus, with an infinite potential for creativity.

Personality, which is soul, cannot exist apart from mind, so every personality must be the expression of some mind. Mortal man has been married to the carnal mind for so long that we actually think that we are in charge of our own lives, but this is not so.

The carnal mind is the Tree of the Knowledge of Good and Evil. She expresses both good and evil in a variety of degrees and combinations through the personalities (bodies) that she is joined to.

The thoughts of the carnal mind, which are divided against one another, become walls of separation because ***good*** and ***evil*** are opposing character traits. Christ Jesus is the Tree of Life, which consistently expresses righteousness through the personalities (bodies) that He is joined to. His thoughts flow harmoniously through them all.

What is perceived as ***individuality*** down here in the lower heaven, but is really the divisive qualities of the carnal mind, fades away in the upper heaven. Each personality is an individual in the upper heaven because she is a unique, creative expression of the perfect man, Christ Jesus.

The individual, but harmoniously flowing personalities (bodies) of Christ, are that great, new city, the Holy Jerusalem, where all those who are living out of Christ Jesus meet and share spiritual experiences . . . .

Rev 21:2

> ² AND I JOHN SAW **THE HOLY CITY, NEW JERUSALEM**, COMING DOWN FROM GOD OUT OF HEAVEN, PREPARED AS A BRIDE ADORNED FOR HER HUSBAND. **KJV**

. . . she is the bride, the Lamb's wife . . .

Rev 21:9-10

> ⁹ AND THERE CAME UNTO ME ONE OF THE SEVEN ANGELS WHICH HAD THE SEVEN VIALS FULL OF THE SEVEN

LAST PLAGUES, AND TALKED WITH ME, SAYING, COME HITHER, I WILL SHEW THEE **THE BRIDE, THE LAMB'S WIFE**.

[10] AND HE CARRIED ME AWAY IN THE SPIRIT TO A GREAT AND HIGH MOUNTAIN, AND SHEWED ME **THAT GREAT CITY, THE HOLY JERUSALEM**, DESCENDING OUT OF HEAVEN FROM GOD, **KJV**

. . . and she is the body of Christ Jesus, the many-membered, subconscious mind of the whole New Man that the Lord Jesus, is bringing forth.

Rev 3:14

[14] AND UNTO THE ANGEL OF THE CHURCH OF THE LAODICEANS WRITE; THESE THINGS SAITH THE AMEN, THE FAITHFUL AND TRUE WITNESS, **THE BEGINNING OF THE CREATION OF GOD**; **KJV**

We begin to be baptized into the collective body of Christ when the Spirit of the Lord Jesus, who is above, joins with the resurrected Christ in us.

It does not matter whether you are a Jew or a Gentile, bond or free, male or female. When the resurrected Christ in you joins with Jesus, who is above, Christ Jesus will pierce through your carnal mind and force her underneath Himself. After that, she will not be seen any more. Only Christ Jesus will be seen. This is the Baptism into Christ. Christ Jesus is swallowing up everything that is not of His life.

One Spirit

1 Cor 12:13

[13] . . . AND HAVE BEEN ALL MADE TO DRINK INTO **ONE SPIRIT**. **KJV**

Every personality that expresses Christ Jesus is drinking of the same Spirit of Christ.

Verse 14 says . . .

1 Cor 12:14

> [14] FOR THE BODY IS **NOT ONE MEMBER**, BUT MANY.
> **KJV**

The body of Christ consists of individual personalities (souls) of like mind, who are harmoniously integrated with Christ Jesus within themselves. The body of Christ does not consist of the many physical bodies who attend a local Church.

Christ is the Fulfillment of the Law

Gal 3:22-27

> [22] BUT THE SCRIPTURE HATH CONCLUDED **ALL UNDER SIN**, THAT THE PROMISE BY FAITH OF JESUS CHRIST MIGHT BE GIVEN TO THEM THAT BELIEVE.

Believe what? The Gospel of Perfection.

> [23] BUT BEFORE FAITH CAME, WE WERE **KEPT UNDER THE LAW, SHUT UP** UNTO THE FAITH WHICH SHOULD AFTERWARDS BE REVEALED.

Before Christ began to be formed in you, you were under the law, because Christ is the fulfillment of the law. The Holy Spirit is not the fulfillment of the law. Christ in you is your only hope of being glorified.

This Scripture is speaking about the faith of Jesus Christ, which is Christ in you, your only hope of being glorified . . .

> ²⁴ WHEREFORE **THE LAW WAS OUR SCHOOLMASTER** TO BRING US UNTO CHRIST, THAT WE MIGHT BE JUSTIFIED BY FAITH.

. . . the faith of the Son of God, who is living His life through you.

> ²⁵ BUT **AFTER THAT FAITH IS COME,** WE ARE NO LONGER UNDER A SCHOOLMASTER.
>
> ²⁶ FOR **YE ARE ALL THE CHILDREN OF GOD** BY FAITH IN CHRIST JESUS.
>
> ²⁷ **FOR AS MANY OF YOU AS HAVE BEEN BAPTIZED INTO CHRIST HAVE PUT ON CHRIST. KJV**

We are under the law until Christ in us *becomes the controlling factor of our life*. But, to the best of my knowledge, even those of us that are hungering and thirsting for the life of God, can still walk out from under Christ's will.

I disobey Christ from time to time, and I am not even able to tell you why. Christ is very important to me and He does control a lot of my life. But I must admit that He is not the sole, controlling factor of my life. Sometimes I still listen to my carnal mind.

The Race Against Death

Rev 14:20

> ²⁰ AND **THE WINEPRESS WAS TRODDEN WITHOUT THE CITY,** AND BLOOD CAME OUT OF THE WINEPRESS, EVEN UNTO THE HORSE BRIDLES, BY THE SPACE OF A THOUSAND AND SIX HUNDRED FURLONGS. **KJV**

I have heard many messages preached on this topic. But when we looked up every Greek word of this Scripture, we found that it is talking about the race that Paul said we were all running.

<u>Heb 12:1</u>

> [12] WHEREFORE SEEING WE ALSO ARE COMPASSED ABOUT WITH SO GREAT A CLOUD OF WITNESSES, LET US LAY ASIDE EVERY WEIGHT, AND THE SIN WHICH DOTH SO EASILY BESET US, AND **LET US RUN WITH PATIENCE THE RACE THAT IS SET BEFORE US**, KJV

Where is this race being run? The personality that is joined to Christ Jesus is running a spiritual race while their body is still in this physical world.

The Scripture is saying that the Holy Spirit, Christ, and the Lord Jesus, who is above, are becoming the controlling factor of this fallen, physical world. At the time that this Scripture comes to pass, this world system, which we know as hell, will be like heaven.

The promise of Jesus Christ, or to be like Jesus Christ, is given to them that believe. Believe what? Believe that what happened to Jesus Christ can happen to them also. This is the Gospel of Perfection, that we shall be baptized into His life.

Little Children, Young Men, Fathers

Baptism into Christ occurs when the seed of the Father, (which is imparted through Baptism in the Name of the Lord Jesus) overcomes the carnal mind. The seed of the Father is given to form Christ in us, so that Christ can overcome our carnal mind. That is the Baptism into Christ.

<u>Gal 3:27</u>

> [27] FOR AS MANY OF YOU AS HAVE BEEN **BAPTIZED INTO CHRIST** HAVE PUT ON CHRIST. **KJV**

Here is a cross reference.

1 John 2:13

> [13] I WRITE UNTO YOU, **FATHERS**, BECAUSE YE HAVE KNOWN HIM THAT IS FROM THE BEGINNING. I WRITE UNTO YOU, **YOUNG MEN**, BECAUSE YE HAVE OVERCOME THE WICKED ONE. I WRITE UNTO YOU, **LITTLE CHILDREN**, BECAUSE YE HAVE KNOWN THE FATHER. **KJV**

Verses with words written in a sequence are frequently written from a spiritual perspective. You might say, as they would be seen from above the firmament. This physical world that we live in is the opposite, a mirror image of the spiritual world above. The sequence is out of order for us, so we have to reverse it.

To make sense out of this verse we have to say, *I am talking to you little children because you have known the Father, and I write to you young men because you have overcome the wicked one, and I write to you fathers because you have known Him that is from the beginning*. We are still carnal, and need to reverse the sequence to understand it.

Little children speaks about the personalities that Christ is being formed in, *young men* speaks about the personalities that Christ is maturing and overcoming the carnal mind in, and *fathers* is speaking about the personalities where Christ is married to Jesus above.

You are a father when you possess the virile seed that can impregnate a fallen man with Christ. This is what Peter did in our previous discussion of the lame man. We do not have to stand up here with a microphone when we have a relationship like the one that Jesus had with the Father. The chances are that the Lord will have you preaching, but that does not have to be the case. The important factor is that He is literally living through you.

If God sends you to someone on the subway, or on a bus, and Christ stirs up in you and talks to that person, and that encounter results in Christ being conceived in them, you are a father.

The whole idea of having an altar call and telling people to receive Christ in their heart is spiritual childishness. There is no way you are going to receive Christ in your heart unless **HE** chooses to enter into you. If He did enter into your heart when you answered an altar call, it was because He honored your faith.

Ninety percent of the people who answer an altar call fall away. Why? Because they may have received the Lord Jesus, but He never received them. The Holy Ghost has to seize you, and when He seizes you, you begin to experience His life.

Who do you think you are, carnal mind? Who do you think you are? You are nothing. The Lord has been telling me for years that we are Mickey Mouse. We are mice, all dressed up with bow ties and pretty dresses and deodorant sticks. We are nothing. Make a decision for Christ? How ridiculous! Repent, and ask Him to receive you, and when He does, you, who were nothing, become something.

One God

We have been taught that the Father dwells in His Christ. If you have the Father, you have the Son. What is the difference between the Father and the Holy Spirit?

The Holy Spirit is the Spirit of the Son. The Spirit of Christ is the Spirit of the Father and the Son.

Matt 28:19

> [19] GO YE THEREFORE, AND TEACH ALL NATIONS, **BAPTIZING THEM** IN THE NAME OF THE FATHER, AND OF THE SON, AND OF THE HOLY GHOST: **KJV**

When Jesus said this, He was speaking about two different Baptisms: The Baptism into Christ and the Baptism with the Holy Spirit.

Jesus said, ***baptize them in the name of the Father and the Son,*** which is Christ.

The Lord Jesus Christ was speaking about the two mature baptisms here. He was not speaking about Water Baptism, nor was He speaking about the Baptism in the Name of the Lord, which imparts faith, or conception. He was speaking about putting on Christ, which is permanent full stature, and the Baptism with the Holy Ghost, which is temporary full stature.

Jesus was talking about the two baptisms, which are the final stages of His perfected creation. This very important point puts a big hole in the doctrinal error known as ***the Trinity.***

There is only One God, and His Name is One.

Deut 6:4

> [4] HEAR, O ISRAEL: **THE LORD OUR GOD IS ONE LORD: KJV**

This means that ***the Father and the Son*** signify One God who is relating to humanity from two different positions:

    (1)   The Father, Who is so far above humanity that He is incomprehensible to us, and

    (2)   Christ Jesus, the Son who we can relate to because of His human experience.

A good example would be to say that our arm (the Son) connects our hand (our humanity) to the rest of the body (the Father), but the arm and the body are parts of the same whole, which is one body.

When the Lord Jesus is appearing as the Father, He is one with the Father, and He is the Father to us, and when the Lord Jesus is

119

appearing as Christ Jesus, He is the Son. So God reveals Himself through the different members of the family of God.

1 Tim 2:5

> [5] FOR THERE IS ONE GOD, AND **ONE MEDIATOR** BETWEEN GOD AND MEN, THE MAN CHRIST JESUS; **KJV**

Therefore, the Scripture teaches that there is only one Mediator between God [the Father] and humanity, [and He is] the [spiritual] man, Christ Jesus [the Son].

God, the Father, abides in the spiritual world above the firmament, *the upper heaven*, and the Son, abides in the earth of *the lower heaven* (the spiritual aspect of man). The Lord is One God who identifies His position in relation to man with Names. The Scriptures that are commonly used to support the doctrine of the Trinity were added to the original manuscript of the Book of John when it was translated from Aramaic.

The View From The Other Side

Baptism into Satan

Luke 22:3

> [3] **THEN ENTERED SATAN** INTO JUDAS SURNAMED ISCARIOT, BEING OF THE NUMBER OF THE TWELVE. **KJV**

Satan is the unconscious part of the carnal mind. Judas was fully baptized into Satan. We can *receive*, or be *filled* with Satan, as well as with the Holy Ghost, because the spirit that rules our mind baptizes us. Satan is the spirit of our carnal mind, so whenever we are in our carnal mind, Satan is present.

Job 1:6

> ⁶ NOW THERE WAS A DAY WHEN THE SONS OF GOD CAME TO PRESENT THEMSELVES BEFORE THE LORD, AND SATAN CAME ALSO AMONG THEM. **KJV**

Jesus told Peter that – for that moment – concerning the present thought in his mind, that he was thinking and speaking Satan's thoughts.

Matt 4:10

> ¹⁰ THEN SAITH JESUS UNTO HIM, **GET THEE HENCE, SATAN**: FOR IT IS WRITTEN, THOU SHALT WORSHIP THE LORD THY GOD, AND HIM ONLY SHALT THOU SERVE. **KJV**

1 Tim 5:15

> ¹⁵ FOR SOME ARE ALREADY **TURNED ASIDE AFTER SATAN**. **KJV**

Our thoughts come from Satan when we are in our carnal mind, and they come from God when we are in our Christ Mind. That is right, our thoughts can come from Satan, even after we have received the Holy Ghost.

Jesus and John were not calling the Pharisees names when they said they were vipers. They were saying that the Pharisees (who claim to be in Jehovah's image), have the Serpent's nature, just like the rest of the world. They have either received, or are baptized into Satan. Whoever has Christ, has received an additional mind.

The peoples of our world are a mixture of good and evil, but only a small minority are ***Satanically evil***, like a serial killer, for instance. Satan and the carnal mind are the Tree of the Knowledge of Good and Evil.

We all have the potential to do evil because of our inherited sin nature, but the extent to which we actually *do* evil deeds, depends upon many factors. Wherefore, Jehovah has given us Christ to save us from our sins.

As soon as Christ is present, He begins to override the Satanic Baptism and controls our carnal mind for increasingly longer periods of time. The more mature we are in Christ, the more Christ controls our carnal mind. However, we can still be influenced by Satan, our unconscious mind, whenever Christ is not controlling her. This is a hard word, but the truth will set us free.

TABLE OF REFERENCES

1

1 Cor 1:30 95
1 Cor 10:2 28
1 Cor 11:19 57
1 Cor 12:10 .... 71, 73
1 Cor 12:13 .... 111, 113
1 Cor 12:14 114
1 Cor 12:28 71
1 Cor 12:30 76
1 Cor 12:4-7 62
1 Cor 13:1 .... 67, 70
1 Cor 13:8-12 69
1 Cor 14:22 .... 73, 74
1 Cor 14:23 73
1 Cor 14:24 75
1 Cor 14:25 75
1 Cor 14:39 78
1 Cor 15:14 89
1 Cor 15:18-20 89
1 Cor 15:20 88
1 Cor 15:22 85
1 Cor 15:29 103
1 Cor 15:3-4 84
1 Cor 15:5 87
1 Cor 3:11 34
1 Cor 6:17 40
1 John 2:13.................... 117
1 Peter 1:2 .... 14, 15

1 Peter 1:9..................... 100
1 Peter 4:12.....................55
1 Peter 5:8.......................99
1 Tim 2:15 61
1 Tim 2:5 .... 15, 120
1 Tim 5:15 121

2

2 Cor 10:4..........................99
2 Cor 11:3..........................92
2 Cor 5:2,4.........................23
2 Peter 1:19.....................86
2 Peter 3:10.....................96

A

Acts 1:5.............................52
Acts 1:8.............................60
Acts 10:2,4........................32
Acts 10:30-31 32
Acts 10:38.................... 7, 70
Acts 10:38-39 52
Acts 10:44............ 30, 52, 63
Acts 10:44-45 59
Acts 10:45........................54
Acts 10:46............ 54, 71, 72
Acts 10:47.................. 33, 59
Acts 10:48.................. 33, 64
Acts 13:9-11 41
Acts 19:4................... 11, 27

Acts 19:5 .... 27, 30
Acts 19:6 .... 30, 46, 72
Acts 2:2 20
Acts 2:4 .... 62, 71
Acts 3:2 109
Acts 3:4-5 109
Acts 3:6 108
Acts 3:7-8 108
Acts 4:30 61
Acts 8:18-19 45
Acts 9:17 81
Acts 9:17-18 83

C

Col 1:18 26
Col 1:27 .... 25, 45, 96
Col 3:10 .... 14, 15

D

Deut 6:4 119

E

Eph 2:15 90
Eph 4:13 .... 7, 77, 84
Eph 6:18 78
Ezek 14:3 58

G

Gal 2:20 25
Gal 3:16 46
Gal 3:22-27 114
Gal 3:27 116
Gal 4:19 31
Gen 1:16 86
Gen 1:5 86
Gen 2:21 90

Gen 24:3-4 56

H

Heb 12:1 116
Heb 12:29 95
Heb 2:10 104
Heb 6:19 102
Heb 6:2 38

J

James 1:21 .... 31, 107
James 2:17 99
James 4:7 21
Job 1:6 121
John 1:42 87
John 12:34 104
John 20:12 89
John 20:17 89
John 4:35 36
John 6:63 106
John 8:58 85
John 9:4 99
Jude 20-21 78
Jude 3 98

L

Luke 10:2 37
Luke 22:3 120
Luke 24:46 84
Luke 3:38 .... 16, 90
Luke 3:7-15 20
Luke 8:5-8 28

M

Mark 1:1 91
Mark 16:14 87

Mark 16:16 97
Mark 16:17 .... 68, 71
Matt 13:8 18
Matt 17:2 92
Matt 28:19 118
Matt 3:11 .... 17, 95
Matt 3:11-12 18
Matt 4:10 121
Matt 5:15 65
Matt 5:48 97

P

Phil 3:8 58
Phil 3:9 35

R

Rev 1:5 85

Rev 12:1-2 79
Rev 12:4 ....40, 61
Rev 12:5-6 79
Rev 14:20 115
Rev 14:4 42
Rev 21:2 112
Rev 21:9-10 112
Rev 3:14 113
Rom 1:4 103
Rom 6:3-9 101
Rom 8:11 39
Rom 8:26 76
Rom 9:6 18

T

Titus 3:6 91

ABOUT THE AUTHOR

Sheila R. Vitale is the Spiritual Leader, Founding Teacher, and Pastor of *Living Epistles Ministries (LEM)*. She moves in the offices of Teacher of Apostolic Doctrine, Prophet, Evangelist and Pastor, has an international following, and has been expounding on the Scripture through a unique spiritual lens for nearly three decades.

She has written more than 50 books based on the Old and New Testaments including *Ephraim, Man of the Earth and The Eagle Ascended (OT), and Salvation* and *Not Without Blood (NT)*. She has also rendered original spiritual interpretations of Biblical texts such as *The Woman in The Well (John, Chapter 4)* and *First Corinthians, Chapter 11*. Her unique, Multi-Part Message style is seen in *LEM* Serial Messages such as *A Place Teeming With Life* (9 Parts) and *Quantum Mechanics in Creation* (18 Parts). Each Part of a Multi-Part Message Series can also be enjoyed as a complete and independent study. In addition, she has defined, explained, illustrated and demonstrated hundreds of spiritual principles throughout more than 1,000 *LEM* Lectures.

Her signature work, however, is the three volumes of *The Alternate Translation Bible (ATB)*: *The Alternate Translation of The Old Testament, The Alternate Translation of The New Testament* and *The Alternate Translation of the Book of Revelation. The Alternate Translation Bible* is a work in progress (*The ATB Project*). Accordingly, additional spiritual interpretations of both whole and partial Chapters are added from time to time, as they are rendered. The most up-to-date versions of *The ATB Project* may be found online at *The LEM* Website (*LivingEpistles.org*). *The ATB* is a *spiritual interpretation* of the Scripture and is not intended to replace traditional translations.

She also analyzed the Greek text of *The Book of Revelation* and preached extensively on it in the early years of *The ATB Project*. During that time she produced 197 distinct *Message Parts*, under 29 specific *Message Titles*, all of which deal with *The Book of*

Revelation. Also, many of her books such as, *Adam and The Two Judgmen*ts and *A Study in Unconscious Mind Control*, have been translated into Spanish, as well as *The Book of Revelation.*

Pastor Vitale is an illustrator of spiritual principles, a researcher, a translator and a reviewer of the Modern Social Trends of Family and Culture, as they are revealed through TV programs (*The Sopranos),* movies (*The Matrix* and *The Edge of Tomorrow)* and plays *(Wicked).* She also writes for the *LEM Blog.*

She travels domestically, as well as internationally, preaching and teaching Judeo-Christian Spiritual Philosophy, and has donated Audio Libraries of her Lectures to other ministries in Africa, Asia, Europe and North America,

Pastor Vitale serves *LEM* in a range of spiritual, educational, and administrative functions from *The Selden Centre*, *LEM* headquarters in Selden, New York. She is also a philanthropic individual who supports the *Lighthouse Mission (Patchogue, NY) and HGM – Mission of Hope – Haiti, and other* charitable organizations. She also supports community services such as the *Terryville Fire Department.*

In her spare time, Pastor Vitale enjoys watching movies, attending plays and partaking of cuisines from different cultures. An avid traveler, she has visited several countries in Europe and Africa as well as many cities in the United States.

BEGINNINGS, INSPIRATION AND CALLING

Pastor Vitale began her spiritual journey as a child when her Jewish mother enrolled her in the Hebrew school of an Orthodox synagogue. She experienced the Spirit of God for the first time there in such a profound way that she wept. But after that, when she was only eleven years old, she became very ill and was taken to Mount Sinai Hospital in New York City. She almost died there and has battled with life-threatening health issues ever since. Nevertheless, a deep longing for God continued to pursue her until several years later when she desperately wanted to attend Yeshiva (Jewish high school), but could not. Her secular parents approved of her choice, but could not afford the tuition.

Much later, after years of searching, she once again experienced the Spirit that had brought her to tears in the synagogue of her youth, but this time it was at *Gospel Revivals Ministries*, a Pentecostal church where Deliverance Ministry was emphasized. She had a desire to understand the Bible since she was a child, but Scripture was difficult for her and she struggled with the text. Nevertheless, she read one Chapter of the Bible every day until, one day, *her spiritual eyes opened* and she saw an angel holding a little book.

After that, she attended as many as five teaching services each week for about seven years, the latter part of which she edited *Pastor Holzhauser's* books. But several more years had to pass before *the eyes of her understanding opened even further* and she began to receive *Revelation Knowledge of the Scripture*. She understood at that time that the angel she had seen was the angel of Revelation 10:8.

After about seven years of learning *Deliverance Ministry* and *The Doctrine of Sonship (Bill Britton)* from *Pastor Holzhauser,* she studied the Bible independently under the influence and direction of the Holy Spirit.

In **1998** she began teaching Apostolic Doctrine.

In **1990** she spent three months in Stony Brook Hospital where she recovered from an incurable disease, defeating premature death, once again, and went on to resume teaching and managing *LEM.*

In **1992** she journeyed to Africa for the first time, where she was called to the office of Evangelist.

In the **mid-1990s,** she began to Pastor in addition to being a Teacher of Apostolic Doctrine, a Prophet and an Evangelist, thus, satisfying all five offices of *The Ministry of the Lord Jesus Christ to His Church*.

LIVING EPISTLES MINISTRIES

Pastor Vitale was happy fellowshipping at *Gospel Revivals Ministries* but, eventually, she desired a deeper and more spiritual understanding of the Word of God. One day, after crying out to Jesus about her need, she was amazed to hear Him ask her if she would teach. Her initial response was that she did not see how it would be possible since she was already working a full-time job, despite her poor health. But after the Lord asked her for a second and then a third time, she reluctantly agreed, believing that He would empower her to do the job. Shortly thereafter, in the latter part of 1987, she began to teach her own brand of Judeo-Christian Spiritual Philosophy.

The Lord Jesus Christ named the work *Living Epistles Ministries* in 1988.

The first *LEM* meetings were casual and spontaneous gatherings of friends and fellow deliverance workers in Pastor Vitale's home. After that, they were held in the business office of one of the brethren. Pastor Vitale delivered her first formal message entitled *The Truth About Witchcraft in January of 1988*, followed by *The Seduction of Eve* in April of the same year. After that, she prepared and taught weekly messages including *Signs of Apostleship* and *Lazarus & The Rich Man. The meetings eventually* increased to two and then three each week.

Sometime after that, she learned that the Lord Jesus Christ was revealing spiritual principles from the Hebrew text of the Old Testament through her teachings, and she used those spiritual principles to begin to unlock the mysteries of the New Testament, as well. Today she understands that the Scripture is a spiritual document that must be spiritually discerned if it is to be understood correctly, and calls that spiritual understanding *The Doctrine of Christ*.

LEM publishes a wide range of material, including books, e-books, spiritual interpretations of the Scripture and transcripts of many of Pastor Vitale's Lectures and on-line meetings, all of which, as well as the entire *Alternate Translation Bible,* may be viewed free of charge on the *LEM* website (*LivingEpistles.org*). She also has an *Author's Website* where all of her books, as well as several photographs of herself and a short biography are displayed (Amazon.com/author/SheilaVitale). Paperback and digital versions of *LEM* books may be purchased through *Amazon, Google Books* and *Barnes & Noble.*

LEM provides free video livestreams through YouTube and other Internet Platforms . . .

@LivingEpistlesMinistries (2016 – Sept. 2022)
@LivingEpistlesMinistriesLEM (Oct. 2022 – Ongoing)
@LivingEpistlesMinistries (LEM disciples)

. . . as well as two channels of *Shortclips* where short, focused messages of about 15 minutes each are posted:

@shortclipsbysheilar.vitale3334 (2016 – Sept. 2022)
@ShortClips-SheilaVitale (Oct. 2022 – Ongoing)

LEM donates a significant percentage of its income to other Christian ministries and organizations that advocate for Christian values and defend the United States Constitution.

PASTOR VITALE TODAY

Today Pastor Vitale continues to dedicate her life to teaching the spiritual principles of the Bible and focuses daily on studying, writing and preaching powerful messages from *The Selden Centre,* LEM/CCK's headquarters at Selden, New York.

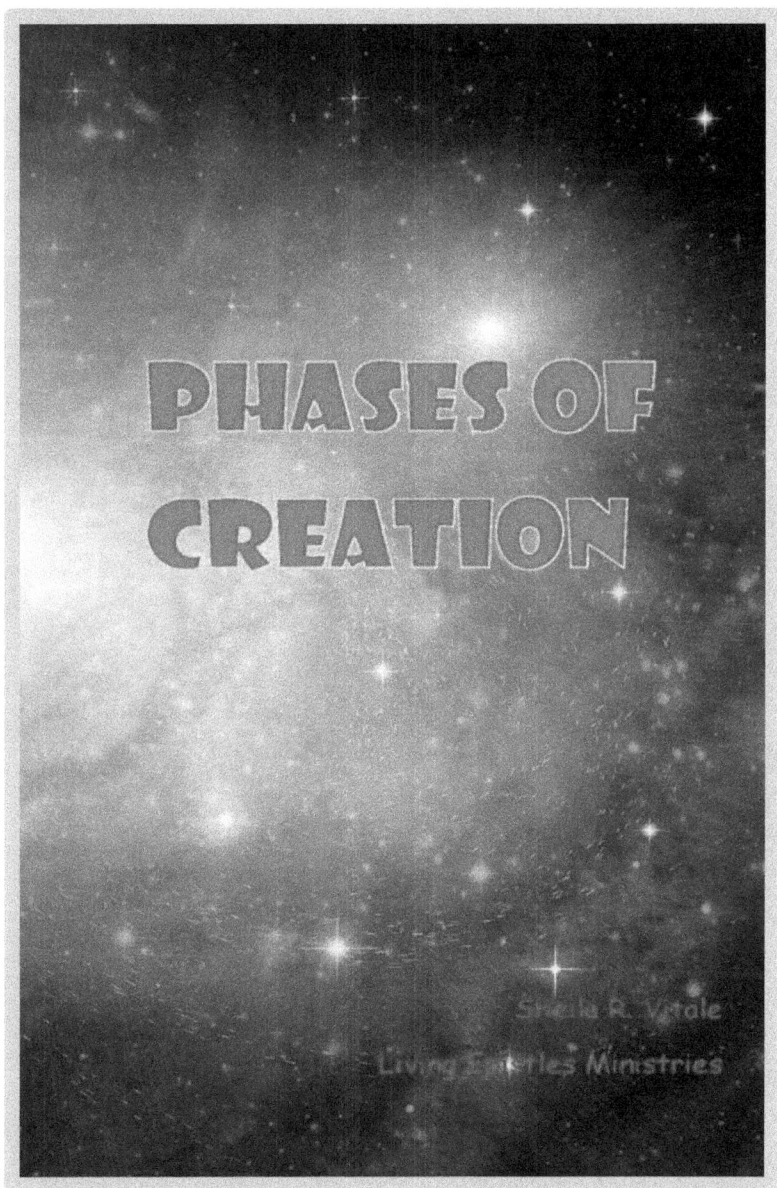

PHASES OF
CREATION

Sheila R. Vitale
Living Epistles Ministries

Phases of Creation has two distinct sections. The first Section is an esoteric treatise on creation. The second Section deals with deception in the Church

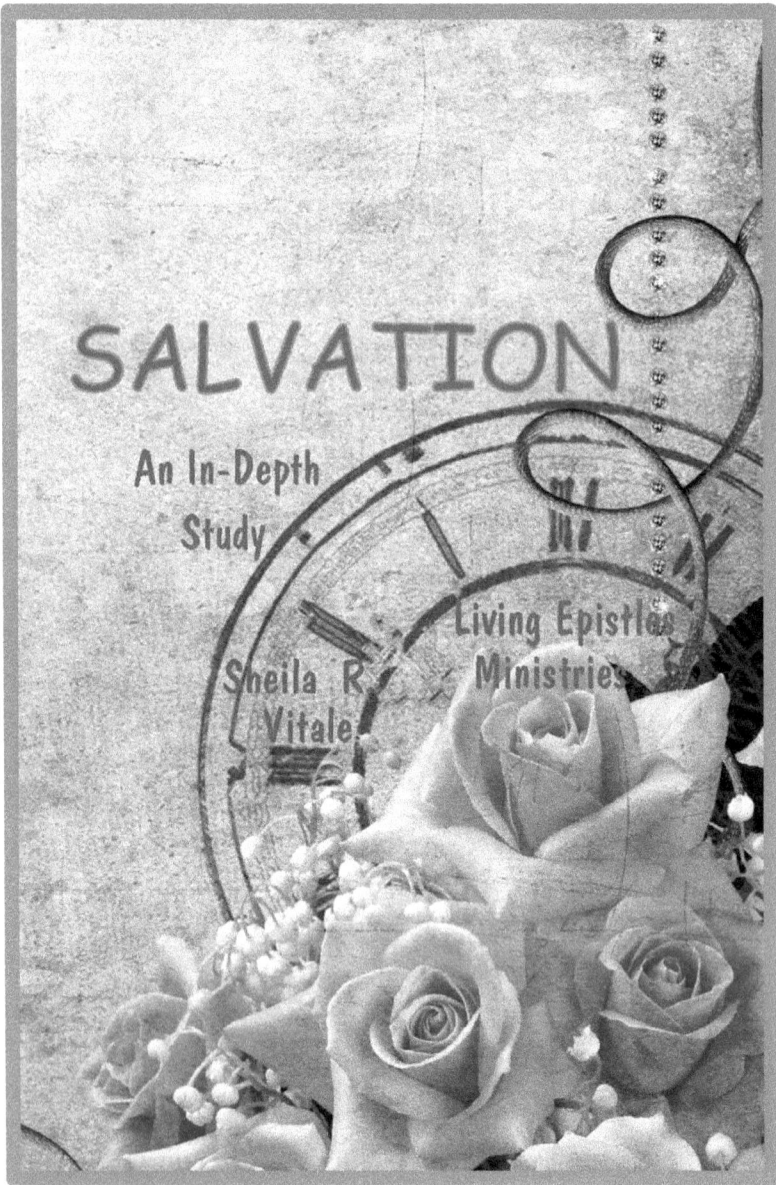

Salvation is an in-depth study which includes Redemption, Sanctification, Adoption and Forgiveness, as well as some insight into Salvation for Israel.

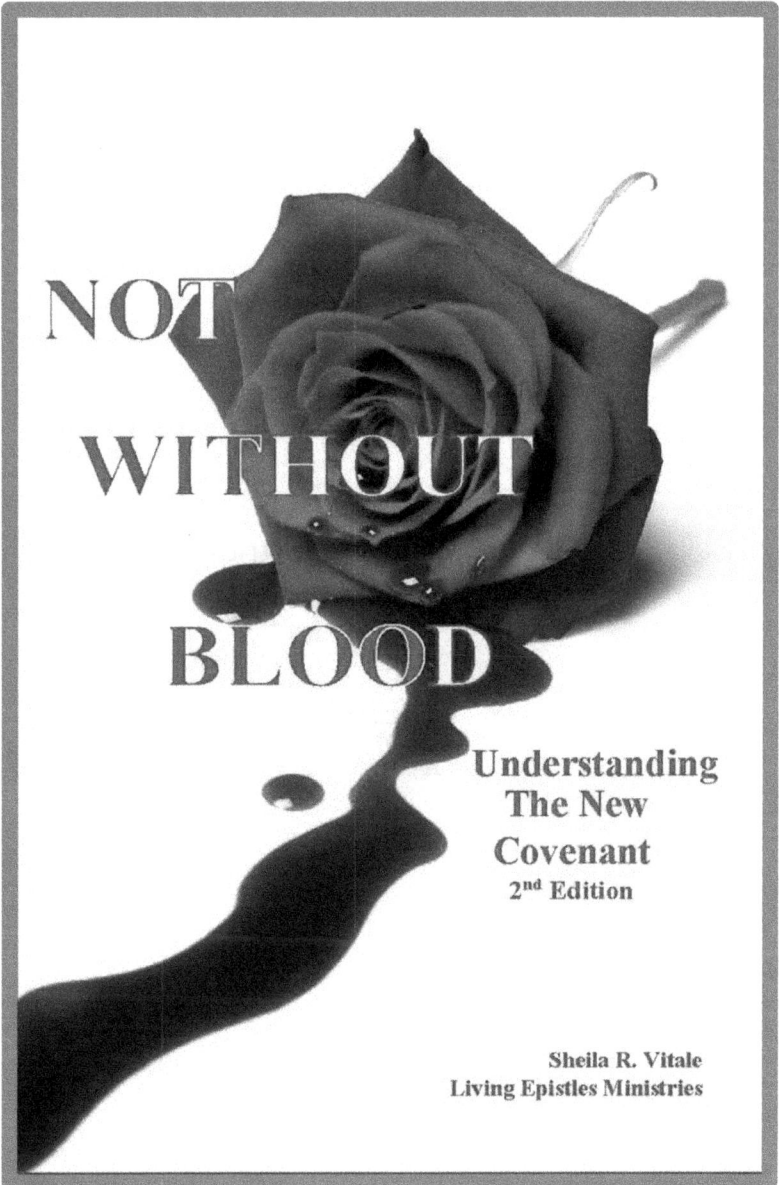

Not Without Blood explains that Jesus' sacrifice gained access to the throne of God for all mankind, but that each individual must offer up his own sin nature in exchange for Jesus' righteousness nature.

Living Epistles Ministries

Sheila R. Vitale

Pastor, Teacher & Founder

Judeo-Christian Spiritual Philosophy

PO Box 562, Port Jefferson Station, New York 11776, USA

LivingEpistles.org

or

Books@LivingEpistles.org

www.ingramcontent.com/pod-product-compliance
Lightning Source LLC
Chambersburg PA
CBHW070808100426
42742CB00012B/2291